Charlie &
Skowhei

ALASKA TRIP

Cath & I.

61 (2818)

Le Nora Corbele
Eagle Trail Ranch

# WIND ON THE WATER
*The Story of a Pioneering
Alaskan Couple*

# WIND ON THE WATER
## The Story of a Pioneering Alaskan Couple

by LeNora Huntley Conkle
as told to Jim Rearden

Great Northwest Publishing
and Distributing Company, Inc.
Anchorage, Alaska
1991

*Dedication*
*Dedicated to the memory of my husband, Clement M.*
*"Bud" Conkle, Alaska Master Guide, 1912–1985, and my*
*son, Richard Lloyd Huntley, (1930–1987), who came to*
*Alaska with us. We have no reason to feel any sorrow for*
*them now; only ourselves for having lost them.*

*Acknowledgements*
*I am thankful to Mr. Jim Rearden for his kind assistance*
*in bringing this project to fruition.*

# CONTENTS

9

# *I*

## TANADA LAKE

If there is a lovelier place in the world than Tanada Lake, in Alaska's great Wrangell mountains, I don't know where it is. My first view of this six-mile-long mountain-backed body of water that the local Indians call "Wind on the Water" came one winter when my husband Bud and I lived at Rufus Creek, on the Nabesna Road, then a narrow, winding, improved trail that led from Alaska's Tok Highway some 40 miles to an old gold mine.

It was one of those glorious March days when winter had begun to relax. Daylight hours were increasing, the biting winter temperatures had eased, and, a few miles to our east—sometimes seemingly within arm's reach—the great Wrangell Mountains soared into the blue sky. Bud, on snowshoes, left the cabin after harnessing the five dogs of our team. I was to meet him with the team at Copper River, where his last traps were set.

The dogs were reluctant to work for me, and I had to stand on the brake to hold them back because they wanted to follow Bud. They knew I was an inexperienced musher, and they loved it. After Bud was out of sight I shouted "Mush," in what I thought was a voice of authority. Jim, the lead dog, calmly sat and looked back at me, tongue lolling, a big grin on his face. I used a few of the cuss words I'd heard Bud use with the dogs, but Black Boy, the wheel dog (next to the sled) and Wooly, the swing dog (just behind the leader) followed the example of Jim, the lead dog. I didn't

Sawing lumber.

Dad and "papoose."

dare turn loose of the handle bars, knowing they would probably bolt immediately. After a time Jim half-heartedly headed out the trail. Each dog hoisted a leg in turn on each bush, and repeatedly looked back to laugh at me. We poked along until we met Bud, returning to see what was taking us so long. He had checked all his traps and was half way back when we met.

"You've got to be tough with them, LeNora," he said. "Where's your switch?"

I didn't have a switch, and the dogs knew it.

Bud took over the handle bars and called to Jim, "Come haw." Jim swung slowly to the left, but Black Boy stood, feet braced. He growled when Bud approached him with a willow switch.

"You think because you bluffed LeNora you can do the same with me?" Bud calmly said.

I held my breath to see who was going to win. Bud surprised me by kneeling eye-to-eye in front of the big black dog. Suddenly Bud growled loudly and fiercely. Black Boy's tail dropped and disappeared in the crease between his hind legs and Bud had no further difficulty with him that day.

We had planned to travel up the Copper River as far as feasible and camp overnight. It was an area into which Bud wanted to extend his trap line if sign looked good. Ice on the river was smooth and easy going for the dogs and sled, and we traveled on the river, passing through a narrow channel with high bluffs on both sides. From there Bud broke trail across country to Copper Lake, where we set up a comfortable lean-to camp. We cooked dog food, then our steaks, and spent a relaxed evening next to a fragrant campfire, surrounded by the beauty of the mountains. It was a peaceful setting, and we watched in silence as evenings' twilight absorbed the day, watching the last rays of the sun linger on majestic distant Mount Sanford. A lone wolf far off in a canyon sent up a long wailing call, and an answer came from a pack so far off that their cries were barely audible. The tired dogs lifted their heads and stared into the growing darkness, listening. I wondered then, and still wonder: what goes through sled dogs' minds when their not-too-distant relatives call? The moment passed, and the weary dogs returned to their slumbers. We too soon sought sleep as we settled into our warm sleeping bag spread on springy spruce boughs.

During the night we were awakened by a loud booming, crashing, and crunching. It could mean only one thing—ice had gone out of Copper River, the route we had followed to reach Copper Lake, and the one we had planned to follow home. Bud checked at first light and confirmed what we already knew—where we had blithely traveled the previous day, ice was grinding and moving in big slabs, piling up in the narrow channel between the bluffs.

To return home we had to cross five-and-a-half-mile- long Copper Lake, negotiate two miles of low tundra to Tanada Lake, then run down Tanada Lake, leaving us seven miles of travel to the Nabesna Road. Smoke Thomas and his wife Ruth had a cabin near Jack Lake close to the Nabesna Road (which deep snow kept closed during winter), and the sled dog trail from their cabin would be easy going for us on the rest of our trip back to our home cabin at Rufus Creek.

It took Bud all day to break trail in the deep snow from where we were camped to the other end of Copper Lake. We let the trail set overnight to harden so it would make better traveling for the dogs and sled. I remained in camp with the dogs while Bud worked, and had dinner ready when he returned. That night I cooked the last of the dog food. Our two-day one-night trip had suddenly been extended by Mother Nature, and we were short on grub, and not only for the dogs.

While Bud was breaking trail I had gathered dry firewood, and that evening a glowing campfire of logs in front of our canvas leanto warmed us cozily. We did notice that it grew cold as the fire burned down. Twice during the night Bud got out of the warm sleeping bag and built up the fire. We later learned that the temperature dropped to $-40$ F. that night.

"Time to get going," Bud called next morning shortly after daylight.

"Throw another log on the fire, my adventure-loving husband. Then and only then will I get up," I told him from the depths of the sleeping bag. I could tell by my cold nose that if I climbed out of that bag without a blazing fire near, the rest of me would get as cold as my nose.

Bud had broken trail to within a mile of the east shore of Copper Lake, and the dogs pulled the sled with me on the runners most of the way, following close behind Bud as he snowshoed ahead. Occasionally a dog broke through the crust. I too broke through as I tried to walk on the trail without snowshoes. We were all tired when finally we reached the shoreline and made camp near a good wood supply. The dogs rested as we erected our lean-to, then we sat beside the fire to drink our lunch—which was identical to breakfast: two cups each of sweetened tea. I congratulated myself for putting in a full box of tea bags with plenty of sugar. This was a lesson I learned early in our outdoor experiences in Alaska: no matter how short the trip, carry extra tea and sugar. A tea break renews energy.

Bud left with the dogs and empty sled to check snow conditions on the two-mile low tundra stretch to Tanada Lake. I dragged in wood and spruce boughs for our mattress, and the afternoon went fast. As dusk neared I became concerned, for Bud had been gone much longer than I had expected.

Bud told me later that when he left me he found the going fairly good. He gee'd and haw'd the dogs around the occasional scraggly spruce tree, and traveled mostly in open areas between the hills. He pushed on the sled and the dogs pulled. Then he stopped to rest. While still standing on the runners he took out his handkerchief to blow his runny nose—one of the curses mankind must endure when he ventures into Alaska's winter cold. Wise old lead-dog Jim knew the instant Bud took his hands from the sled handles: at that instant a ptarmigan flushed nearby, and the dogs used that as an excuse to explode into a full run, leaving Bud standing in the trail watching the sled carrying his snowshoes and rifle bounce out of sight. Yelling "Whoa!" only exercised his lungs.

Bud's only hope was that the sled would catch on a stub or a tree. He followed, wallowing in the deep snow, cursing the dogs and himself for his momentary lapse of alertness. Wonder of wonders—in half a mile he found the team, with

We hauled lumber by plane.

Aircraft at Tanada Lake Lodge.

the sled jammed against a tree. What a predicament we would have been in had the sled not hung up.

I don't know what he said to the dogs when he caught up with them, which is just as well. On his return trip he tied the dogs, and with shotgun at ready located the ptarmigan that had spooked the dogs. It flushed within range and he neatly knocked it out of the air. Another bird flushed nearby, and he shot that one on the wing too. Another ten or so birds then flushed and flew out of sight.

That evening we ate birds far fresher than packaged chicken from a super market, after roasting them over the fire, for we had no grease to fry them in. We divided the few bones among the dogs, and to each animal Bud explained that sometimes one goes hungry, "But if you work hard and don't ever leave me on the trail again, somewhere down the line I'll see if I can find some bigger bones with more meat on them for you."

The poor dogs coaxed us for food, and looked questioningly at their food dishes, but we could do nothing about it.

Morning came clear and sunny but cold. We soon reached Tanada Lake, which lies in the foothills of one of the world's most beautiful mountain ranges. Great peaks, fantastic glaciers, dense spruce forests, and open rolling hills—true wilderness—surround the lake. At my first view I couldn't have known of the years we would spend there— years of hard work with its accompanying joys and heart- break. Starting with almost nothing we would first laboriously build a log home, and then expand that into a lodge that would attract lovers of wilderness and wildlife from all over the world. After much study of maps, and talks with oldtimers and local residents, we had decided that if we could find a suitable building site at Tanada Lake it would be the perfect place for us to build the Alaskan wilderness lodge we had long dreamed about.

The ice on Tanada Lake was glassy smooth from wind- whipped snow, and I rode in the sled basket while Bud stood on the runners as the dogs joyfully sped three miles to the lower end, where Tanada Creek drains the lake. Smoke Thomas, a winter neighbor, had been trapping around Tanada Lake, and we found his well-traveled dog team trail, making the last part of our trip an easy and swift dash to the Thomas cabin near the Jack Lake trail. We arrived before dark to the aroma of frying moose steaks, which the Thomases happily shared with us. They had plenty of food for our tired and hungry dogs too.

That April, while there was still a frozen trail and snow for the dogs and sled, Bud and I returned to Tanada Creek for two days. We were anxious to go to the upper end of the lake with the dog team, and we wanted to catch with a gill net some whitefish at the outlet of the lake. Smoke Thomas, with his six huskies, accompanied us. Near the lake's outlet we pitched two tents on a bright sunny day, and there was plenty of open water for the two men to set their gill net across the narrow outlet. We then fished with poles and line until we pulled from the icy water three huge-dorsal-finned grayling for supper. The night passed swiftly, and our dreams were filled with speculation on what we find on the morrow.

Bud and Smoke were tending the gill net that had fished overnight and I was clearing breakfast dishes and repacking the grub box. I leaned over to flip a tarpaulin over our sleeping bag when an excruciating pain hit my back. I couldn't stand. I fell prone, afraid to move, knowing that knife-like pain would strike again if I did.

Clearly I couldn't go on. The men wrapped me in a sleeping bag and I was loaded onto Smoke's long sled. It felt to me as if his six dogs moved like greyhounds about to catch a rabbit. The sled tipped on its side and slid along bumping every tree, rock, and obstruction until Smoke got them stopped. I had clung to the slats of the sled floor to keep from being tossed out, and to keep my back as flat and straight as possible. It was all I could do to keep from crying out from the pain.

Bud then securely tied me in, and after that whenever the sled tipped I simply relaxed, hoping I'd get home alive. Dogs just don't cooperate; the rougher the trail, the faster they went. At home finally, I was out of commission for seven days. I was keenly disappointed that we didn't get to explore Tanada Lake. We went ahead with our plans anyway.

In late April with both dog teams Smoke helped Bud haul tools, canned food and staple food in two small barrels with bear-proof lids from the Nabesna Road to the lower end of Tanada Lake. One of the sleds even held an Aluma Craft boat and outboard motor. Everything was cached in a safe-looking place, and covered with brush so that it was hidden from the air as well the ground. Under the overturned boat was a tent, two surplus military canvas cots, and a small Yukon stove.

During the first week of May I went with Bud to Tanada Lake. Snow was largely gone, but the tundra was still frozen and the dogs could pull the sled with a fair load. I walked along easily, following. Occasionally Bud stopped the dogs to wait while I caught up. I even managed to run short distances, a fact that pleased me.

We pitched our tent on a mossy level place near the lake's outlet and close to Tanada Lake. There were sturdy bushes near where we tied the dogs. They could see each other and also watch us, and they seemed content. There was much open water, with muskrats swimming about; within days many ducks arrived from the south. Days were long, sunny, and mild—a treat after the long winter with its short deep cold days. We caught lake trout and grayling for the pan, and explored the shoreline. After a few days we moved camp half way up the lake to a high bank that seemed ideal for a cabin site, with timber for logs near. Our tent was on a well-worn bear trail, but we didn't think much about that until the first night when it snowed lightly. Next morning we found tracks of a fair-sized grizzly where it had followed along the trail, then made a wide circle around our tent. The dogs had had fits of barking during the night, and now we knew why.

Soon we discovered that swampy land lay under the snow banks, and had to look farther. Shortly we found a mossy sunny knoll that faced the distant mountain sheep hills. It was across the mile-wide part of the lake where we had first camped, where the best timber grew. That meant we would

The new super cub, 1958.

have to float our cabin logs across the lake. The snow was gone from the spot, and we sat in the sunshine discussing the cabin we would build here. It all seemed easy and exciting. Dreams are sometimes the best part of living.

We pitched our eight by ten white canvas tent with three foot walls on level ground. My cot fit across the back, and Bud's lay along one side, while the little Yukon wood stove was near the door flaps. Our clothes remained in duffel bags under the cots, and groceries and cans where they would fit. This was to be our home until we could construct something better. We soon found that the tent wasn't water-proof, but we didn't let that bother us.

Almost every day found us across the frozen lake on the timbered bar cutting logs for the cabin. After felling a tree Bud lopped the branches off, then he went on to fell another while I peeled bark on the first. We worked with a rebuilt chainsaw, a double-bit ax, log chains, a come-along or cable hand winch, a peevee, a hand operated log peeler, and our strength and determination. Bud had worked in the woods as a logger in his home state of New Mexico, so he wasn't exactly a greenhorn. He winched the logs out of the woods, rolling them about with the peevee until they were at the lake. When the ice went out he towed them two at a time across the lake with the boat. He then winched them one at a time to the cabin-site a hundred yards up the steep slope from the lake.

Hard work? You bet. Fun? Yes. We were young and ambitious, and we had a goal.

## II

## BUILDING OUR LOG CABIN

I can't believe now, four decades later, how much we accomplished that first summer. A cabin requires a lot of logs, but we were young and energetic and we didn't discourage easily.

It rained every afternoon that first summer. Most mornings arrived sunny, without a cloud in the sky. We would put our military surplus mummy sleeping bags out on a line to air, and head across the lake in the boat to work. Evenings after supper usually found us drying our sleeping bags by the warmth of the tent stove before going to bed. It took time and patience to get the down bags dry enough and warm enough to settle our tired bodies inside so we could sleep regardless of residual dampness.

We cooked on an open campfire much of the time. If it was raining, and especially if we wanted biscuits to go with our fried fish, I sat on my cot and with the round tin top of the flour container as a table, I mixed the biscuits until they were ready for the pan, and handed the pan to Bud who sat on his cot near the stove. He would put them in the tiny oven.

While waiting, he poured himself a cup of mixed powdered milk and drank most of it. Then he would set the cup on the dirt floor. Almost invariably a tiny shrew would venture from under his cot and climb into the cup. Bud would then put his hand over the cup and swirl it, then tip the white foamy shrew out onto the floor and it would scamper back under his cot.

Could it have been the same shrew each time? Or did the other shrews pounce on the milk-saturated one and eat shrew, milk and all? Shrews are cannibals, and they ate their fellow shrews we caught in traps if we didn't empty the trap immediately. Bud always got such a laugh from his pastime that I couldn't scold him about being cruel. There were so many of the little creatures that summer that we had to keep everything in tin containers. Often at night we felt them run across our sleeping bags. I kept my bag zipped tight and always hoped that none would want inside while I was sleeping.

We took turns fishing to supplement our diet with good-eating jumping-fresh lake trout or grayling, and to add a fish to the dog pot to cook with the corn meal that was the staple of their diet. After a time fishing became a chore instead of a pleasure.

"Your turn to get the fish tonight," I'd comment.

"No, I went last night," Bud often said, trying to get out of going fishing.

We later laughed about this, realizing how much money some of our guests paid for the privilege of fishing in Tanada Lake. It wasn't that the fish weren't in abundance, but that sometimes it took longer than we wanted to remain casting into the water, especially on a cold windy or rainy evening after a hard day of cutting cabin logs.

Every three weeks found us hiking for mail and groceries the seven miles across the rough tundra to our Jeep parked on the Nabesna Road. There was no snow for the sled, so with two dogs leading me, and Bud leading two dogs and another running loose, we eventually arrived at the Jeep, crowded all the dogs in, and drove the 25 miles to Slana if it was early enough to do the shopping and collect the mail. Otherwise we stayed overnight at the Rufus Creek cabin, and went on next day. We again stayed at Rufus Creek cabin for a day before heading back to our construction work at Tanada Lake.

As we prepared for these three-weeks-apart trips, we took the tent down, folded it, and put it and its contents up on a cache Bud had built high between three trees that grew close together. He had sawed off their tops, limbed them, and put a band of tin around each to keep climbing critters off and out of our belongings.

Until the lake ice became too thin for safe travel we used the dogs and sled to travel to the lower end of the lake and return. We then used the boat on Tanada Creek, for the ice went out earlier in the creek than in the lake. In order to control the dogs so they wouldn't chase game or stir up one of the abundant grizzly bears in the area, Bud put them all in the boat. I'd also climb in, and then Bud, wearing hip boots would line the boat down the creek where it was too shallow to run the outboard. The dogs loved this boat ride. They sat, red tongues lolling, with an expression on their faces that clearly said they enjoyed seeing Bud do the work on this part of the trip.

If we took a day off from the log work it was to travel to the lower end of the lake with the dogs and sled where Bud would shoot muskrats and stretch the hides for later sale at Slana. He also had beaver traps at various places that he needed to tend. I rode in the sled and Bud on the runners, and it was easy pulling for the dogs on the smooth ice, and they loved the run.

If we left early we could still peel logs for a few hours after our return. As the days lengthened and became warmer, overflow water crept over the ice, with deep pools here and there. Bud seemed to be able to tell just how deep these overflow pools were, and he drove the dogs straight through them. I would ride in the basket and watch ahead, and I was often sure there was no ice under us as the frigid water came up to the sled basket and my bottom was being soaked. At such times I was ready to abandon this method of travel if only the dogs would stop so I could get off.

"We're ok," Bud would reassure, and he was always right, but then, it wasn't his bottom that was getting wet.

Twice on early trips returning to Tanada Lake Bud tried using the dogs as pack dogs, a common and popular summertime use for sturdy sled dogs. He had made packs for each dog that fit just so. But Jim, the leader, thought it was beneath his dignity to carry a pack, and he obstinately refused to move with a pack on his back. He would simply stand still no matter how far ahead we went, or if Bud touched him a bit smartly with a willow switch.

Keno's legs buckled, and even when Bud lifted him to his feet they collapsed again. Wooly was a small dog and his coat was so wooly that the pack wouldn't stay on his back. Big, strong, and capable Black Boy and the other dogs didn't mind the packs, but went swimming with the flour and sugar in their packs. Bud was the biggest dog, and carried as much as 85 pounds in his pack, and he frequently also carried a five-gallon can of gasoline in each hand, so that he couldn't lead a dog. My packs averaged 30 to 35 pounds, and I always carried a book. Often two books replaced an edible if Bud didn't see the extra one and talk me out of taking it.

Bud acquired two heavy-duty bicycle wheels, and he spent hours building a buggy-like contraption for the dogs to pull—a summer substitute for the sled. The thing collapsed on the first trip, putting everything on our backs again.

Six little pothole lakes were on our route from Tanada Lake to the Nabesna road. Bud decided to take advantage of them. We paddled across the lakes, and the dogs pulled the raft the half mile or so to the next lake. This saved our having to walk around the brushy banks of each of these lakes. It was a good idea, but it didn't work: no matter which direction we were headed, when we launched the raft, the wind blew against us! It was more work and slower traveling to paddle that thing across the lakes than it was for us to walk. We went back to the old tried-and-true Trapper Nelson packboards.

Once that June, when the tundra was swampy and the mosquitoes were at their worst, we were struggling the seven miles to Tanada Lake with heavy packs when at dusk we saw three moose silhouetted against the skyline. They ran full speed across the muskeg with graceful long swinging strides, disappearing into the dusk as we stood and enviously watched.

"Wonder how long it would take to train a moose so one could ride it?" I mused. While dreaming of riding a smooth-gaited moose I tripped, lost my balance, and for the third time that day fell sideways into the cold swampy water. I floundered to my feet, got my pack back on, and saw Bud in the distance. I knew he was wondering what was keeping me. My disposition went sour, and my enthusiasm for wilderness was dimmed considerably by the time we arrived at the boat, still more than an hour from our tent home. I tried to convince myself that on the next trip to Slana I would stay at Tanada Lake and let Bud go alone. But by the time we worked another three weeks I was ready to go again, for we had seen grizzly bears on the hillsides around the lake, and we saw their abundant tracks on the beach where they had foraged. I wasn't brave enough to live in the tent alone while Bud was gone.

We made one trip to Slana that summer that wouldn't have been necessary if Bud hadn't gone wild with salt. One day lake trout were biting as fast as the spinner hit the water, and we decided to salt some for winter. We soon had 20 fat four and five-pounders cleaned. Bud filleted them, heavily salting each filet. He then layered them carefully in the large preserving crock we had back-packed in. I murmured something about the amount of salt he was using, but he ignored me. When the crock was full he put it on the high cache.

It was Bud's turn to murmur a few days later when he realized we were near the end of our salt. He thought he couldn't survive without salt on everything he ate: he even salted food before tasting it. Of course we had to make a trip to Slana for salt and other supplies.

On our return we discovered that a wolverine had climbed past the tin on our cache poles and got into our cache. He had dug out some of the top layer of salted fish and apparently didn't care for it, because he did what the nasty-dispositioned wolverines are noted for—he squatted on the crock and fouled all of our nice lake trout. Bud had a few descriptive adjectives as to what he would do if or when he caught that rascal. I'm not fond of salted fish so I wasn't too sympathetic, but I did wish I could have seen how the wolverine balanced himself on the rim of the crock in order to make the direct hit that he did.

Bud, Lenora and Colin in mid-1950's.

We had interesting company at various times that summer. Occasionally a U.S. Fish and Wildlife Service float plane would land and we would enjoy the visitors. We would learn the latest happenings around the Territory (Alaska became a state in 1959) over cups of coffee and sometimes fresh-baked cinnamon rolls or cookies. Usually it was Ray Woolford and Frank Chapados. Ray is gone now, but Frank still lives in Fairbanks. At the time they were wildlife enforcement agents. They took our letters to mail, and they were always happy to make a phone call or two for us. Later on Bob Burkholder, a FWS predator control agent, was a frequent visitor. In our isolation, visitors became friends, and the news they brought formed a bond of friendship. When an airplane landed, the coffee pot was automatically put on the fire to perk—a familiar symbol of welcome, and a message to the visitor that we wanted him to return. Hospitality is a necessity to people who live in the bush, although most choose that lonely life, and bush living keeps one busy every hour of every day. Nevertheless it is nice to enjoy the friendship and the news that comes with visitors.

In 1951, for $31.50 we ordered from Sears Roebuck a battery-powered Silvertone Farm Radio. The nine volt battery, almost as big as the radio, cost $9.95 plus $3.37 shipping from Seattle. Bud rigged a high antenna in a nearby spruce. We had good reception especially from radio station KFAR, Fairbanks. This station sent radio messages to rural Alaskans via the program they called "Tundra Topics." Thus if a friend planned to fly to Tanada Lake for a visit, KFAR might announce, "Joe Smith and a friend plan to visit the Conkles at Tanada Lake next Friday. They will have with them the repaired outboard motor the Conkles are expecting."

Thus we learned of a pending visit, and, of course, so did everyone else in Interior Alaska. Tundra Topics messages were aired morning and night, immediately after the news, and we listened faithfully and frequently received messages from friends or heard messages to folks we knew or at least knew about. It was like having a party telephone line. We limited ourselves to the news, Tundra Topics, *Gangbusters* and one or two other favorites, because leaving the radio on for any length of time drained the battery. That battery was heavy, and we didn't want to do without our radio news, nor did we want to backpack another battery the seven miles to the lake. By being frugal we found that a battery lasted all summer, until a fresh one could be brought in by dog sled after freeze-up instead of on Bud's back.

Life gradually changed. Minor events sometimes made a world of difference in our lives. The clear bubbling ice-cold spring we found near our cabin thawed so we no longer had to chop ice away to get water. The lake ice melted around the shoreline first, and soon we could use our boat and motor to cross the lake to work on logs. Wind pushed the ice ashore, and I was fascinated to hear it make the tinkling sounds that glass-ice makes when it moves.

For a time we used the rubber raft to cross open water from shore to the still-thick ice in lake's center; we then walked, pulling the raft, then again used the raft to cross open water to shore. After logging and log-peeling all day we returned the same way.

On June 22 we saw the last of the ice on the lake, and Bud got busy towing logs to our cabin site with the outboard motor. He had logs that were twelve inches at the butt all creosoted, pegged into place and leveled, with hand-hewed poles in slots twelve inches apart for floor joists. Would we have a cabin by Christmas?

It was so beautiful at Tanada Lake that on some calm clear days I found it difficult to not simply idle on a hillside with binoculars watching the wildlife, or watching the ever-changing colors on the hills and mountains. On stormy days the clouds and colors presented a fantastic show. The hills across the lake from our cabin changed colors with every passing hour of every day. There were greens, rust brown, and every shade of lavender, with dark shadows in the gullies. Occasionally a band of white Dall sheep, ewes and their frolicking lambs, grazed in the high greening meadows. These were the lambs we had spent hours in May watching when they emerged from the caves on the steep ridge sides which their mothers had entered a day or two earlier to give birth. They were but a few hours old when we first saw them, and on wobbly legs they could bounce and romp on narrow ledges and steep rocky hillsides, giving us endless hours of amusement.

By late November we had a 12 × 14 cabin ready to move into. A double canvas over poles was the roof, and the floor was a variety of widths and lengths of hand-hewn boards. We walked cagily on this floor, for a mis-step meant a board would flip up and slap you smartly from behind; they were not nailed to the pole floor joists. It was a temporary arrangement, until we could replace them with smooth boards. We also had two three-foot-square plastic-covered windows.

I cannot express our happiness at being able to move into our own little log cabin after living through the summer and fall in the crowded tent. The tent had been a challenge to survival as winter progressed. Ever climb out of bed to stand on the frozen ground to dress when the temperature is far below zero? This we did for many weeks while we were completing the cabin enough to make it livable. Once we were moved in, the cabin seemed luxurious and unbelievably spacious with our few belongings in place.

At last, at the expense of some of the hardest work either of us had ever done we had a start on our dreamed-of Alaska wilderness lodge. The path to that time and place in our lives had been long, sometimes difficult, always interesting. I considered myself a small town and big city girl, having lived in Los Angeles, San Francisco, and San Diego. I often shook my head in wonder at finding myself in the great lonely—Alaska's wilderness. In time I shed my longings for the city and became one with Alaska and its wild places. But it took time, a loving husband, and much soul searching.

It all began in San Diego with a hitchhiker.

## III

## THE BEGINNINGS

I was born in an insignificant small farming town—the two Model-A-Ford-size town of Hazelton, Idaho, near the Snake River. I lived most of my growing-up years in Idaho, graduating from high school at Boise. I was second from the top in the J.D. Quint family of ten children. We were so poor that even the poor folks called us poor. No one in my family hunted, but we always had healthy things to eat. I learned how to care for babies, sew, cut hair, milk a cow, garden, and do all-round chores and to get along with what was available. It was make-do or do without in my early years—a philosophy that perfectly fit my life in Alaska in later years.

I was healthy and athletic and enjoyed any and all activities. I swam summers, ice skated winters, and played basketball in high school. Soon after graduating I married young and moved to California. The marriage lasted only long enough to produce three babies, and suddenly I found myself raising them alone.

I have never had an aversion to work and I was always able to find a paying job to keep my children fed and the rent paid. Nor was I too proud to clean houses for others for pay.

In time I found better paying work sewing, and I worked myself up from being an employee to owning my own upholstery, furniture slip, and drapery business. I contracted drapery and furniture slip cover sales for Sears

The big new sign at Tanada Lake Lodge.

Roebuck and three of the noted interior decorators in La-Jolla. It was a lucrative business, my kids were more than half grown, and my comfortable home was almost paid for. I thought my life was well established.

Then came December 7th, and the Japanese attack on Pearl Harbor. How well I remember San Diego in war time, a city with huge navy and U.S. Marine bases. Suddenly those great battleships and aircraft carriers that we had scarcely glanced at as they sailed in and out of the bay assumed a new importance, and everyone's eyes were on them. San Diego changed overnight into a war city, with sailors, marines, and soldiers crowding into town for training and shipment overseas. War work started up at such plants as Ryan Aircraft—the little factory that in 1927 built Charles Lindbergh's *Spirit of St. Louis.*

I was driving my 1938 Ford sedan back to San Diego from a day's work at LaJolla and saw two U.S. Marines in their olive green uniforms hitchiking from Camp Pendleton to San Diego. In wartime no hitchhiking serviceman ever had to wait very long for a ride: the hopes and prayers of the nation rested on these brave men, and though my mother had taught me to never pick up strangers, I picked up these two. The marine wearing his garrison cap at a jaunty angle did all the talking, and the two had no place in particular to go: they were looking for a change from their base routine.

I happened to mention the horse my daughter owned, and the riding club where she and I and some navy wives went horseback riding Sunday mornings. That gave the jaunty-capped marine, who turned out to be a New Mexico cowboy, a foot in the door. He insisted that he had to accompany me home to see that horse, and he had to have my telephone number so he could go riding with us Sunday mornings.

That marine was Clement M. "Bud" Conkle. He easily remained aboard my daughter's horse—a horse that normally preferred to have only my daughter or me on his back. He also showed off with some fancy trick riding. Marine Conkle impressed my kids and all the neighbor kids who always seemed to congregate at my house. I must be honest and say that the kids were more impressed than I was. But my boys were willing to give up their bed so the two marines could stay overnight so they could accompany us riding the next morning. I then drove them back to Camp Pendleton and forgot about them. But Conkle didn't forget. He returned for many weekends to go horseback riding. We talked of horses and many things, including Alaska. Bud was determined that he was going to live in Alaska after the war. He wanted to build a wilderness lodge for hunters and fishermen. His enthusiasm was contagious, and one day I rashly promised, "Sure, I'll go to Alaska with you when the war is over."

That was the day he came to say goodbye because he was being shipped overseas. So many of our fighting Marines were not returning from overseas at the time that I hardly thought twice about my promise: it didn't seem likely that it would happen. We were facing a long hard war.

Too, I was 32 years old, settled in a successful career, and I had many obligations. How could I pull up roots and move to a wild and unsettled land like Alaska?

While he was overseas Bud wrote me many letters, and in most of them he talked about his dreams of Alaska. I dutifully wrote back, becoming more and more attached to the man and his dream. Bud fought in the Pacific while I continued my life as it had been. And then the war was over, and in January 1946, after serving for four years, Bud was discharged from the U.S. Marine Corps. His last duty as a marine sergeant was with the occupation forces in Japan. Then suddenly, he was back in San Diego, afire with plans to move to Alaska.

I couldn't say no. I married Bud in April 1946 and two months later our two-wheel trailer was hooked to our new civilian Willys Jeep, ready for the road. Our neighbors gathered to wish us well on our journey. We planned to drive to Seattle and ship the Jeep and trailer to Alaska on a steamer. Daughter Fay waved goodbye, not knowing when she would see us again. At age 14 she had no desire to go to Alaska. However my 16-year-old son, R. Lloyd Huntley was to accompany us. We had burned our bridges, even though not one of us had been to Alaska. We had read so much about it that our confidence was high.

We wended our way through the high desert country of Southern California, arrived at Lake Tahoe, and crossed to Clear Lake in northern California, then drove on through Oregon and to Seattle, where we looked for a ship that would take our Jeep, our trailer, and us to Alaska. It was late May, and the earliest we could get passage for the Jeep and trailer was "sometime in July."

We couldn't wait. We tried to learn if the Alcan Highway (now called the Alaska Highway) was open to civilians and drivable. No one knew. Someone said we would have to get permission from Canadian authorities in Edmonton to drive the Alcan. We decided to push on and take our chances on driving the Alcan; we might be turned back, but at least we'd go see.

There was no red tape at the U.S.-Canada border. The agents were friendly and wished us well on our drive to Alaska. In Alberta we talked with many people in little towns and along the road. We preferred to buy groceries at little country stores and in so doing we learned that lots of cars were traveling to Alaska. We repeatedly heard of a truck traveling a few days ahead of us; it was said to be loaded with a dairy cow and chickens.

We lived from the land as we traveled. Eggs from a farmer cost thirty five cents a dozen. We camped nights, fighting mosquitoes, cooking over a Coleman stove. Often we camped near streams where we caught trout to augment our diet. Our first gasoline in Canada cost thirty five cents an imperial gallon. Our trailer was too heavily loaded for the half-worn-out tires that were available after the war, and we had flat tires seemingly by the dozen. We had three before we left California, two in Oregon. In a small Oregon town Bud talked a man out of two tires that were on an unused trailer parked in his yard. When we hit gravel roads in Canada the flats and blowouts increased. For a time we averaged either a flat or a blowout every 20 or 30 miles. Fortunately we had a generous supply of tire patches. Bud bought a new tire for the trailer in Canada.

At Edmonton, Gateway to the North Country, and Heart of the Prairie, we checked into an auto court, bathed, and washed clothes. At the government office that issued travel permits for the Alcan Highway we found several people in line ahead of us before the doors opened on a Monday morning. Our wait was short, and the red tape minimal. I never did figure out why the men in that office wore kilts.

"Do you have enough funds, spare parts, and tires to get you through Canada?" we were asked.

"Yep," answered Bud.

"Have a good trip," offered the official.

We had to get visitor's ration stamps to buy meat and butter, and along with the butter we bought a ham and bacon, as well as a full sack of bananas. Butter hadn't been available in San Diego for three years, and bananas hadn't been in the markets of San Diego for two years.

We left Edmonton in high spirits, headed north. Four hours later the metal trailer tongue cracked, and we limped into a small town and waited hours to have it welded.

My old diary reveals that on June 5 we traveled across the flat prairies of Alberta all day, shot a rabbit, and fried it for dinner. We found a big truck tire beside the road and sold it to a service station for $20, making us feel that we didn't lose so much after all on the two Canadian tires we had purchased for our trailer for $417. They hadn't lasted 300 miles.

We took the wrong road that day, for to us all the farm roads looked alike, and signs were few and far between. We came to a settlement where everyone spoke French. No one seemed to know which road we should take to get to Dawson Creek; in fact, those we tried to talk with acted as if they had never heard of Dawson Creek. We gave up asking and drove in a northerly direction and about ten o'clock that night camped in a burned-over draw close to a creek. It wasn't a good camp, but we were too tired to look farther.

Next day we followed the narrow old trail heading north. In the morning we saw school kids with lunch pails coming from farm lanes and being picked up with a horse-pulled buggy. School buggy? The kids all stared at us strangely, and didn't wave back at us.

We finally emerged from the country road we had mistakenly taken to find the "highway" to Dawson Creek—a muddy trail with deep ruts. The trailer tongue cracked

Lenora and Colin at Tanada Lake.

again, so we slowly and carefully drove on to Spirit River where we waited for hours in the hot sun and dust for it to be re-welded.

While Bud was overseeing that project, Lloyd and I browsed through the local trading post where we bought and ate a sack of bananas. That night we camped on a branch of the Peace River, nine miles from Dawson Creek, the true beginning of the Alcan Highway. Mosquitoes tried to eat us alive, and smudge fires didn't discourage them one bit.

We reached Dawson Creek on June 7. While Bud had our travel passes for the Alcan checked, Lloyd and I bought more bananas, and we saw goodies in the stores that hadn't been available for several years in war-time San Diego. At the Blueberry Hill checkpoint 100 miles from Dawson Creek a sergeant glanced at our outfit and nodded us on. After reading so much about American troops building this road through the wilderness it was exciting to be on it, to see it firsthand. We were proud of our country for the tremendous undertaking, and it was a double thrill to be on a well-built highway, even though it was gravel, after the rough and rugged Canadian roads. We passed abandoned Army barracks from time to time and thought of the rugged kind of frost-bitten and mosquito-plagued life our boys had had while living in such ramshackle buildings as they worked long hours pushing the highway through.

Topping a curve we had a breathtaking view of the Peace River valley, and a huge bridge spanning the river. Bud remembered that this was the bridge that the wind had destroyed at Tacoma Narrows, Washington. It had been salvaged and hauled piecemeal to this lonely site. The Alaska Highway, of course, was built under emergency wartime conditions in order to provide a supply route for the defense of Alaska.

As we rounded another curve we came upon a very large bull moose. He stood looking at us as Bud brought the Jeep to a sudden stop, then he eased into the timber and was nowhere in sight by the time we were out of the Jeep for a better look. At dusk a large black bear sauntering alongside the road ahead, stopped, stood on a log and looked over his shoulder at us where we had stopped. Then it too disappeared into the woods. Our days were exciting, for there was potential adventure around every bend.

On June 8 we awoke to frost on the ground and ice in the water bucket. We had listened for the howl of wolves, but all we heard was the angry buzzing of mosquitoes outside our nets. We drove all day on a fine road with tall spruce trees alongside. Once a gray timber wolf crossed the road ahead and disappeared into the timber. Late in the afternoon we followed an old side road to a run-down log cabin that had not been occupied in ages. We camped in a lovely grove of trees near a clear running stream, a fork of the Racing River near McDonald Creek at Mile 415½. I fried potatoes and made biscuits in a Dutch oven, Lloyd chopped firewood, and Bud caught enough grayling for supper. After supper we all went fishing. Grayling struck as soon as the spinner hit the water. We saved what we needed for breakfast, but kept fishing for fun, releasing all the uninjured fish.

Next morning the fishing tempted us again. I was watching Lloyd fight an 18-inch grayling that was putting up a good fight.

"There's a bear, Lloyd," I said in warning, as a bear appeared on the opposite bank.

"It's only a black bear. It won't hurt us," he reassured me. He had his pistol, just in case. The bear didn't appear to be interested in us, but I stayed close to Lloyd, ready to dash for camp if it started to cross the stream.

Suddenly a big fish hit my lure and gave such a jerk that I turned and tripped over branches but got onto my feet again with the fish still on. A second bear came out of the woods to join the first. That did it. I was definitely ready to leave, but by the time I landed my 20-inch grayling they were gone. Lloyd was enjoying the fishing too much to be concerned about a couple of black bears, but Bud scolded us for not returning to camp immediately. He knew that black bears can be dangerous.

We loved the long daylight hours. We were still cleaning fish at 11 p. m., and it was just starting to grow dark; the sun rose at 3:30 in the morning. Wonderful!

We talked with fellow travelers. Some had "Alaska

Bound," or "Alaska or Bust," written on their cars. Most were heavily loaded, as we were, with household goods, tools, camp gear. As we drove we saw an occasional Indian camp beside the highway, and sometimes we saw the poles of a fish camp by a river.

We pulled into the tiny community of Watson Lake one late evening and gassed up, which meant that we pumped gasoline out of a barrel into our Jeep, and filled the jerry cans we carried. While refueling we talked to several men who were waiting for a bush plane to fly them to a new gold strike on the Firth River. Later three men arrived and arranged to leave their pickup truck—they too were catching a plane to Yellowknife where the strike was reported. Exciting. Life in the Far North was exceeding anything we had read or dreamed about.

At Watson Lake a white man and his Indian wife with three little girls drove up in a dilapidated Ford pickup and went into the trading post. The little girls had piercing black eyes, and straight jet-black hair. They didn't smile, nor did they show any childish curiosity in what was going on about them. Were they exceedingly shy? Frightened?

We browsed in the trading post and were fascinated by the huge black wolf pelt a trapper had brought in. Items for sale included wood stoves, axes, snowshoes, woolen clothing, packboards, sled dog harness, raw furs, hardware of various kinds. The mixed odors of raw skins, oil, and wool seemed foreign and exotic.

We drove on and drove down a faint trail leading to a stream where we found an abundant supply of mosquitoes. Smudge fires didn't slow them a bit. We rushed through setting up camp and cooking and eating supper, and found blessed relief inside mosquito nets and sleeping bags.

At Whitehorse we stood in awe of two old paddle wheel river steamboats, especially the *Yukoner*. They were weather-worn and appeared permanently beached. There was a time when such sternwheelers were the glory of the Yukon River, hauling passengers and freight, stopping along the way to pick up firewood for their boilers. We walked on the board sidewalks of this frontier town, and gawked at the mostly log buildings and homes.

Canadian Mounted Police, wearing smart brown uniforms with yellow stripes down the sides of their pants told us about the folks with the cow and chickens in their truck. When they unloaded the cow to milk it at Whitehorse, half of the town turned out to watch. Many had never seen a cow. The kids knew only milk from a can.

Canadians love their horses, and we saw beautiful horses free on open range along highways all through Canada. Motorists had to be alert, for the animals frequently trekked along the roadways. We reached beautiful, huge, Kluane Lake, and followed around its shores for 35 miles, with snow-capped mountains mirrored in the clear blue water. We were each lost in our dreams as we drank in the splendor of the scenery, when Wham! another trailer blowout. Patched it again. Patches on patches. Shortly a grizzly bear ran across the road in front of us. I yanked the coat that Lloyd had over his sleeping face so he could see it, but the bear was gone by the time he woke up. A Jeep tire got low and Bud stopped to pump it up. The operator of a passing road grader stopped to sympathize, and told us that the road was much better in Alaska.

Soon a roly-poly fat little black bear ran beside the road, wanting to cross. Bud kept the Jeep even with it, and soon its red tongue was hanging out. Bud felt ashamed and slowed down to allow it to leap across the road and disappear among the trees. Then the tire Bud had just repaired started to bulge, so he replaced it with a well-patched spare, and we searched for a campsite, tired and ready to quit for the day.

We crossed the border into Alaska on June 15. We were so excited at seeing the "Welcome to Alaska" sign that we drove right by it, forgetting that I had kept one last picture on our last roll of film to make a photo that had so much meaning to us. The road was much wider and smoother, and we drove late, looking for a camping place. We stopped once near Big Delta, but the mosquitoes were so thick and fierce that we leaped into the Jeep and felt fortunate to escape with any blood left.

At 1:30 a.m. we finally stopped near Shaw Creek, just south of Fairbanks. Lloyd sat up to watch to see if the sun disappeared during the night. We learned, of course, to take the long daylight hours in stride, and enjoyed watching the sun seem to circle around us during a 24 hour day in mid-June, dipping briefly below the horizon near midnight.

Talk about friendly people! Everyone waved as they drove by, and a man and his wife stopped to ask if we had mosquito dope because they had seen us vigorously slapping at the pests. We didn't of course, and they gave us a bottle of 6–12 repellent that the army was issuing to soldiers. It worked! They were also generous with the "friendship-jug" they carried. Shortly a truck full of U.S. Army boys stopped to talk: they had been swimming at a lake down the road.

During the night and early morning the sky resounded to the beautiful sounds of wild geese honking. They had nesting grounds on the nearby Tanana River and among the hundreds of lakes and potholes in the Tanana Valley.

We had fried rabbit for dinner; actually snowshoe hare. The cycle was high, and rabbits were everywhere. Dozens and dozens of them appeared at the gravel pit where we camped. While we were eating, a saucy squirrel with a lot of nerve helped himself to a chocolate-covered cookie from our open chuck box. We laughed at its frustration when it tried to get the cookie out of the cellophane bag. When it succeeded, it flipped its bushy tail at us, scolded us for laughing at him, then sat on a log and ate all the chocolate off. The sun had melted the chocolate, and the comical little rascal had melted chocolate all over its whiskers, nose, and paws.

We were a little disappointed with the stunted black spruce, the swampy, flat, muskeggy look as we neared Fairbanks. However the sun was shining brightly, and our spirits were high with the challenge of new adventure, and perhaps the end of our journey if we liked Fairbanks well enough to stay a while.

We drove into Fairbanks just five weeks after leaving San Diego, and immediately found the post office with mail from home. We ate lunch in what we later learned was a long-time fixture in Fairbanks, the Model Cafe on Second Avenue. We then drove two miles to a gravel pit near the meandering Chena River. We weren't long in discovering that we had picked the best place for a super abundance of mosquitoes. Our only escape was under mosquito nets.

We drove around Fairbanks, discovering it had some beautiful homes, many old log homes, no skyscrapers, and some rundown areas. It had a frontier feel to it that we liked, and there was a relaxed atmosphere and a leisurely approach to life that was a refreshing change from San Diego.

I look back with fond memories. If I had known what I know today, on that June 17, 1946, I'd have written something like this in my diary:

Fairbanks, Alaska, here we are. We're cheechakos (greenhorns) now, but we will learn and adjust. Soon we'll know enough to make camp where a breeze keeps mosquitoes down. We'll learn the place names of the rivers, the mountains, the Indian and Eskimo villages. We'll experience the deep cold and short daylight days of winter. We'll glory in the freedoms and challenges of our last frontier, and we will become a part of this vast and glorious land. We will also find that dreamed-of place of beauty in the wilderness where we will build our hunting and fishing lodge. But first we must serve our apprenticeship; we must become Alaskans.

*IV*

## OUR FIRST SUMMER

Good things quickly happened to us at Fairbanks. The day after our arrival we straightened our camp, put on clean clothing and drove around town enjoying the old log cabins and wondering who lived in the more modern frame houses. Bud recognized a man he had talked with briefly and we stopped to chat. The man worked for the Army at Ladd Field, and told Bud he was sure Bud could get work there too.

"I'll be there first thing tommorrow," Bud said.

That evening while we were preparing supper a man stopped at our camp and asked Lloyd if he wanted a job. He was foreman on a job at Big Delta, 100 miles from Fairbanks on the Alcan Highway, and was returning there in two days.

"Sure, I'd love to have a job," Lloyd said after he heard what the wages were. They were far above what a boy Lloyd's age could normally expect. Lloyd was tall, strong, and willing, and the job didn't require any special skill, only a willingness to work and learn.

Next morning Bud went to Ladd Field (now renamed Fort Wainright) adjacent to Fairbanks to look for a job and was immediately put to work. The war's end had left many businesses in the Fairbanks area short-handed, and the economy was booming. To us the wages seemed astronomical. Next day Lloyd left for Big Delta. With Bud gone with the Jeep, I stayed in camp to care for our camp and equip-

Tanada Lake Lodge going up.

ment. I rushed through my cleanup and spent most of my time stretched out on my cot under mosquito netting reading *Forever Amber*, a steamy romance of the time.

It was a good time to read. The sun was hot, and the energetic mosquitoes had voracious appetites; they sat on the netting saying, "She has to come out of there some time; we'll get her then." Even resting a toe, knee, or elbow against the netting meant itching welts. We soon purchased new bottles of the 6–12 insect repellent and I'd paint it all over my net and clothes. Dust stuck nicely.

We attended a late movie one evening and experienced the strange sensation of leaving the darkened theater for bright daylight. Then back to our tent home and the buzzing insects awaiting their feast of blood. It's too messy to put dope on for a few minutes only to have to wash it off before going to bed, so we suffered.

Bud arrived home early one afternoon and we went house hunting. No luck. We met many interesting people though. Housing was unbelievably tight in Fairbanks. We returned to our tent camp still hopeful that we'd soon find a decent roof to put over our heads. Our camp was not very far from one of the two local dairy farms, that of Charlie Creamer. Wild geese fed in his fields, and they flew over our camp in the early morning. Their honkings and V-formations were a thrilling start to every day.

We enjoyed June 21, the longest day of the year. It was almost considered a holiday in this land of the midnight sun. There were boat excursion, and a baseball game played—at midnight, of course—by the Midnight Sun League. It sounded like fun, but we had important work to do: we were moving to our next home, an old converted bus. It was much roomier than the tent. There were screens on the windows and we could move around comfortably and didn't have to use mosquito nets over our cots.

The bus belonged to one of Bud's fellow workers at Ladd Field, and was on his homestead at mile six of the Richardson Highway. A neighborly friend, an old-timer in the area, Jess Davidson, used his Caterpillar tractor to move the bus to level ground for us. I scrubbed and cleaned it and we moved in.

We continued to search in Fairbanks for a suitable house, for the bus wouldn't do for winter. I wasn't looking for a job, but I got one anyway. A nice little shop on a side street had a sign, "Interior Decorating and Gift Shop." I was curious, for it was the type of work I had done in California. I talked with Margo Bailey, the young owner and learned she was just getting started, but already had many orders for drapes and slip covers, and needed someone to do the sewing. It was work made to order for me, and she asked me to start work immediately. We had hauled with us in our overloaded trailer my heavy-duty sewing machine, and I put it to work.

Before I could start sewing though I had to unpack and wash or take to the cleaners all my clothing. Dust had filtered into every box, bag, and corner of our trailer. I washed by hand and had to carry the water too. We took showers at Ladd Field, a blessing. Bud set the tent up outside the bus for storage. We had no clothes closet, so we made do, hanging clothes here and there. We had a small table and two benches and a box on which we set our battery-powered radio. While I did all this Bud got involved in helping a neighbor disk his field when he got home from work and after supper. The long daylight hours encouraged us to work far longer hours than we ever had.

On July 4th Bud and I fished the Salcha River, a few miles from Fairbanks, without catching anything. We returned home too tired to clean up and go to the street dance and celebration in Fairbanks. It sounded like fun, but we had to be at work early in the morning.

The following weekend we drove the 100 miles to the Delta Clearwater where I caught four big grayling, 20 and 21 inches long, real beauties. Bud didn't catch anything and he didn't appreciate my bragging about who was the best fisherman. We stopped at Big Delta to visit with Lloyd. A friend from his school days in San Diego was also on the job, and they were pals. He liked his work.

Our next home was a three-room cabin on a homestead. Rex, the owner, a single man, was away on a job until winter, and he had offered us the cabin while he was gone. I spent a few evenings cleaning. We installed new linoleum on the floors, and I hung curtains, and it was quite homey. It wasn't anything like the modern home I had left in San Diego, but for frontier living it was fine. Bud spent hours trying to remove sand from the water pipes so the pump would work. It was hopeless and he had to give up and we carried water from the nearby creek.

We received a telegram from my daughter Fay that she would be arriving on the plane from San Diego. We rushed to finish moving, then met her at the airport. She had blonded her hair and wore a blue suit. I was startled at how much she had grown up in such a short time, but happy to have my daughter with me again.

Bud built a tent frame with a wood floor and pitched the tent over it, giving us good storage.

A friendly old-timer with a nearby homestead frequently visited us. We always stopped everything to listen to his stories of early gold mining in Alaska. He personally knew many of the famous early day bush pilots, and other pioneers we had read about.

Fay and I spent evenings picking wild blueberries which grew in abundance everywhere. We canned some, made pies and jellies, and ate them by the bowl-full with canned milk and sugar. Next came the wild cranberries, tart, tiny, and delicious when made into sauce.

One Saturday night Fay and I drove the Jeep the six miles to Fairbanks to go to a movie and, surprise, we bumped into Lloyd. He had just arrived from Big Delta and hadn't had time to find us yet. He had only a short time in town, then had to rush back to his job which he was enthused about.

We planned a weekend fishing trip. The chuck box was loaded with food, and we pitched sleeping bags, fishing gear, and a small tent into the Jeep. Fay had everything ready to go when we returned home from work, so we left immediately. Fay accompanied us, although she wasn't an enthusiastic camper.

We drove up the Steese Highway north of Fairbanks, toward Circle City, enjoying the lovely scenery. We stopped to take a close look at huge floating gold dredges working near the highway. Fireweed was in full bloom with its deep red hues; and many other flowers grew in profusion along the highway.

Late that evening we found and drove into a dim trail that had been described to us as a fine place to fish. We built a cozy campfire and I cooked a nice supper while Bud made a mattress of spruce boughs and unrolled our double size sleeping bag near the Jeep. We zipped Fay into a mummy sleeping bag in the front seat of the Jeep and went to sleep.

We had been warned of the many bears in the area, so Bud had his rifle near. A year earlier a man had disappeared nearby, and searchers had found only one of his shoes— with a foot in it. We went to sleep confident that Bud could handle any bear that might come into camp. Suddenly we were awakened by a terrific commotion. It sounded like a bear trying to tear the Jeep apart. Bud, rifle in hand, quickly learned it was only Fay trying to get the zipper of her sleeping bag opened for an emergency exit into the bushes. It took both of us to get her out of that sleeping bag. When she returned from the bushes she refused to allow the zipper to be closed again. Mosquitoes found her, and she was so noisy in swatting them and bouncing around that we decided we might as well get up and start our day.

We had forgotten coffee mugs. Bud soon had some not-too-rusty cans cut to size and the rims smoothed so we wouldn't cut our lips. Of all the things I saw Bud improvise for camping comfort over the years, I never saw him make a cup from a tin can that didn't scorch the mouth before the coffee was lukewarm. I am never enthused about lukewarm coffee, especially for breakfast.

Bud tied a Colorado spinner on his line and went to the creek while I cleaned up the breakfast clutter. Soon Fay and I followed, deciding to wade the stream to find Bud. I wore hip boots, and Fay climbed on my back for me to ferry her across. As we neared the far side both of us were laughing when I slipped and we both fell full length into the icy water. The sun was warm so we sat on a mossy bank drying out and watching a mama duck and her brood swimming about. We were dry when Bud returned with a string of ten grayling. I tried to catch a fish with Bud's pole without any luck. We soon ate our fill of fish fried to a golden brown, with bread and butter. Grayling are white-fleshed and delicious.

Two things bothered me about living in Fairbanks—the heat and the mosquitos. July in 1946 was especially warm for Fairbanks. "Be patient. It won't last," the old-timers told me when I complained about the heat. "They'll be gone with the first freeze," they said of the mosquitos.

We met and visited with the famous Leonard Seppala, one of Alaska's greatest sled dog men. He participated in the famous 1925 diphtheria serum run to Nome. When we met him he lived near Fairbanks and we had a lovely time admiring the lovely Siberian Huskies he was raising. Seppala, a small man of Finnish extraction, was friendly and outgoing, and showed us the many trophies he had won in his races, with photos of many of his dog teams. He gave us autographed pictures of his Huskies that I still treasure.

We learned of a fishwheel that was operating in the nearby Tanana River. One evening we drove to it, but found the wheel was stopped and no salmon in the box. A fishwheel, turned by the current, scoops salmon from the water and deposits them in a storage box. We were disappointed.

We walked downstream and were standing on the bank looking in the water when Bud saw a big bright red salmon slowly working his way upstream. Bud bounded upstream to the fishwheel where he pulled the stick jamming it, allowing it to turn. At the first turn of the wheel the salmon Bud had spotted came up in one of the scoops and Bud turned the wheel by hand to make the fish slide into the holding box, where it lay flopping violently. Thinking the fish might leap out of the box into the water, Bud jumped into the box, intending to grab it. But the salmon grabbed him. It bit him on the leg with its big mouth and teeth and wouldn't turn loose. Bud, angry, yelled for me to run to the Jeep for the hatchet. It was too funny for me to miss, so I stood there on the bank laughing while he pried the salmon's jaws open. The sharp teeth had made red dents in his legs through his jeans.

We had salmon steaks for several meals from that fish and we thought they were pretty good eating. We didn't know yet that most Alaskans don't consider salmon in bright spawnings colors to be especially desirable: the silvery ones fresh from the sea are best.

Lenora on the trapline.

Lenora and Charm the cat.

When we returned home that evening a cow moose and her calf were grazing in our yard. We sat quietly in the Jeep and watched them until they left.

Lloyd's foreman stopped to pick up more clothes for Lloyd. He had coffee with us and told us about "The Boy," which is how they referred to Lloyd. He was learning to run a bulldozer, and had painted a barracks.

"We couldn't tell which was Lloyd and which was the barracks wall. Both were covered with paint," he laughed.

It sounded as if the crew was enjoying Lloyd, which pleased us.

I couldn't share with Bud and Lloyd a firsthand look at Fay learning to take a bath in a round galvanized washtub. I laughingly told them how I had to demonstrate to her how to sit in the tub. She thought it a very crude way to get clean. A terrible way to have to live, she thought—no bathtub with hot and cold running water at the turn of a knob. No lights at the turn of a switch. Fay was born and raised in my modern home. I was surprised that she didn't complain loudly about having to go outdoors to the outhouse. Where I grew up in Idaho for many years I had taken my Saturday night bath in a washtub before I realized that average-income families could afford such luxuries as indoor plumbing, with a toilet in the house. I remember as a kid having the choice of carrying fresh water for my bath, or taking a bath in the same water used by two ahead of me.

A lady I met when making drapes for her new home gave me a full-size rubber bathtub in a folding hardwood frame. It had never been used. I think that my telling her of my daughter's loss of dignity in a round galvanized washtub was what prompted her to give me the tub.

It required many buckets of carried water, although one had the choice of using a little bit of water, or filling the tub. We used that rubber tub for many years.

One weekend in September Bud, Lloyd, and I drove from Fairbanks to Rainbow Mountain, in the heart of the great Alaska Range on the Richardson Highway. In four-wheel-drive with the Jeep we left the highway and followed a bulldozed trail for about five miles and made camp.

Next morning we crossed a wide stream and climbed to a

high plateau. Blueberries were large and thick, and we walked on a heavy carpet of red and green leaves and moss. We dropped our packs and rested and enjoyed a breathtaking panoramic view of the surrounding mountains. With binoculars we found some white Dall sheep ewes and lambs feeding high in the mountains.

After a time we shouldered packs and crossed a deep canyon to explore further. Climbing the steep hillside we stopped to rest on a sunny crest and with binoculars Bud located a huge Dall ram high in the mountains. Soon several smaller rams appeared, and we enjoyed watching their playful antics as they butted at one another. There is a special feeling that comes when one watches wild animals in their own environment when they have no idea they are being watched.

We camped on the edge of a dense spruce forest beside a creek that bubbled over colorful rocks. During the night we awoke to the drumming of rain on the tent. At daylight we crawled from damp sleeping bags, got a warming fire burning, and headed for the Jeep. Fog hung in the mountains and we couldn't tell where we were. The creeks we had easily crossed the previous day were now swollen, and we had to walk far upstream on some of them to find places we could cross. We arrived at the Jeep late, but decided to drive back to Fairbanks anyway, for we were both due at work next morning.

I was driving as we neared Delta Junction when I thought I saw a truck pulling out on the highway with its lights on dim. I slowed, then suddenly realized that I was staring into the light-reflecting eyes of a huge bull buffalo. Previously I had seen buffalo only in a zoo.

I slammed on the brakes and blurted, "Wow! Is this guy going to charge?"

That awoke Bud and Lloyd, who were sleeping.

"Put it in reverse and get out of here," Bud quickly said. "Let him have all the room he wants."

Good advice. We had read about a buffalo bull in this area that had challenged even big trucks on the highway. I'm sure that's the bull we saw. I swiftly backed up and gave the old boy all the room he wanted. The flourishing herd of bison at Delta Junction was started in 1928 with a small transplant from Montana.

The old-timers were right: with the first frosts of fall the mosquitoes mostly disappeared. And it was incredible how swiftly the temperature plunged after the warm summer months. We had met the challenge of summer at Fairbanks. Now, could we handle the famous short days and deep cold of an Interior Alaska winter?

*V*

## WINTER

In January 1947 the temperature at Fairbanks stayed at −50 F. or colder for most of the month. Sometimes the mercury dropped to −60 or −70. That winter Snag, Yukon Territory, registered −83 F. as its coldest. In Fairbanks taxi cabs did a huge business. In order to keep running, cab drivers left their engines idling when not under way. Residents who drove their own cars and who didn't have heated garages—and most didn't—had to heat their engines by various means for at least an hour before they would start. One of the common approaches was to drape a tarpaulin over the engine with a blowtorch blasting heat under the oil pan. This called for constant attention because of the danger of fire.

Many cars driving around town had only peek-holes in their frosted windshield. I was surprised at how few fender-benders occurred. To most drivers the cold was an old enemy, and driving with icy windshields was part of the battle.

Ice-fog—tiny particles of ice floating in the air—existed most of that January. For 28 days that month no mail or freight arrived at Fairbanks. There were no trains much of the time due to huge snowslides on the tracks. When mail did come it often consisted of weeks-old newspapers. The first ships arriving in Valdez carried the high-profit items of beer and whiskey. Groceries and milk had a lower priority. All was trucked from Valdez along the icy Richardson

Bringing home the Christmas tree.

The weasel and sled-going for firewood.

Highway through the Alaska Range to Fairbanks. Freight charges on every item were sky-high; air freight rates were charged even if the items arrived at Valdez or Seward by ship.

The deep dry cold was a challenge to this former resident of Southern California. I found that without putting on parka, boots, or mittens I could walk to the corner cafe from the drapery shop where I worked, or across the street, but no farther. The cold penetrated suddenly. Neither Bud nor I had ever experienced such cold, and I felt we did well. Others survived, and we did too.

Bud's job at Ladd Field was to keep coal loaded and hauled to the many heating units. Keeping equipment running in the deep cold was a constant battle, and Bud learned all of the tricks of the trade—tricks that were later to prove invaluable to us when we were far out in the wilderness and totally on our own.

Before winter set in Bud had asked some of the old-timers how they managed when the temperature dropped far below zero. The usual answer was "We carry on as usual. It just takes longer."

Bud knew if they could do it he could too. Later when it was − 60 and colder some of these old-timers were conspicuous by their absence from the job: they were home by the fire and the younger men, the so-called cheechakos, were on the job.

In December when the temperature started dropping to − 40 Bud frequently got up at night to start the Jeep to keep it warm. When it was − 50 he lost it: the Jeep was not a good starter in the cold, and he didn't have a headbolt heater to keep it warm with electricity all night. When he couldn't start the Jeep he walked to work bundled in Army surplus clothing.

I had use of a steam-heated apartment in the rear of the shop where I worked, and I stayed there when Bud worked nights. Bud would come in from work and sleep a few hours, then spend more hours with a blowtorch under the Jeep until it would start. Then we'd go back to our house to eat dinner and start the work cycle again.

We received an invitation to a New Year party at the

Country Club, a big social affair. I had thought that people stayed home on such cold nights, but we were initiated into the "Fifty-Below-Zero-Club". Everyone arrived in snowsuits or heavy outer clothing—often beautiful fur parkas and fur mukluks. Underneath were dress suits and long fancy evening gowns. I had given away my long dresses when we left San Diego, with the inaccurate remark, "I know I won't wear this in Alaska." It was a fun evening and I realized that established Fairbanksans knew how to enjoy themselves during the long winter months.

"It's the coldest winter, and last summer was the hottest summer, I can remember," many old-timers told us. So we arrived at a great time to be introduced to Interior Alaska. On some mornings as I walked the long two blocks to the post office, if I didn't recognize the eyes that looked at me from beneath a fur cap and scarved face, or recognized the voice that greeted me, I wouldn't have known who the bundled-up person was. On one very cold night Bud walked seven blocks to get me a half gallon of ice cream. He loved it—both the ice cream and the cold.

In February the temperature shot up to above freezing, and everyone who didn't have a freezer and had moose meat hanging outside had to rent meat lockers. We saw a 40 degree change in temperature, from $-20$ to $+20$ within 24 hours. Next day the temperature climbed to above freezing, and water started to drip from the icicles.

We were excited spectators at the North American Championship Sled Dog Races at Fairbanks. Bud met one of the great championship racers, Gareth Wright, and later in the spring he bought three huskies from him—dogs Gareth could no longer use in his racing teams. It didn't matter to us that they were culls from a racing team—we wanted working dogs. Bud eagerly looked forward to bringing his three huskies home that spring. He visited them every chance he had, wanting them to know him. He talked to dog mushers on techniques of handling, harnessing, feeding, and training sled dogs.

By chance Bud purchased a fine dog sled for $40—the amount of money the man happened to need that day. At the time good dog sleds sometimes brought hundreds of dollars. We never did wear that sled out; it was still in perfect condition when we sold it many years later.

We were fascinated with the Black Rapids Glacier area on the Richardson Highway, about 150 miles from Fairbanks. There we met old-timer Charlie Miller, who had a cabin at Miller Creek, 10 miles from Black Rapids Roadhouse, an ancient log establishment that dated to the early 1900's. Twice in March and once in April we drove to Black Rapids Roadhouse, parked there and with packboards, bedrolls, groceries, and Charlie's mail, snowshoed to Trims Camp, a Road Commission maintenance camp that was closed for winter but which had an open room with an oil stove and plenty of fuel. Next day we went on to Charlie's for a day and overnight with him in his little log cabin. Then the long hike back to the Jeep in that beautiful white, winter wonderland, and the drive back to Fairbanks with arrival about midnight.

Strenuous? You bet. And we loved it. Charlie Miller fascinated us with stories of the early days on the Richardson Highway when horse-drawn sleds were used to travel it in winter, and horses and wagons summers. There were plenty of stories of hardships, sudden storms, and lost lives.

Charlie had us convinced that there was a rich gold vein in the little claim he was working by the Delta River. It was, he believed, deep, and he needed a bulldozer to get to it. Bud was a good dozer operator, but we didn't have the bulldozer. We were tempted to give up our plans for a hunting lodge and instead dig for gold. If Charlie had a rich gold vein there by the Delta River, it's still there as far as I know.

We barely escaped having gold fever.

Charlie's second major interest was in winning the great Alaskan guessing game—when the ice went out of the Tanana River at Nenana. Each year the person (or persons) who guess the precise time collects more than $100,000, and Charlie was bound that he was going to win that big purse. He spent hours calculating weather, depth of snow, average temperature, date, hour, and minute the ice had gone out in past years, and I don't know what all.

Charlie was probably in his 70's when we knew him, and he was determined to strike it rich and go Outside (the term for the other states) to live in comfort. We heard later that he did go outside to live all right—at Morningside Hospital, in Washington state. Morningside was the mental institution where in those years Alaskans who left the tracks were sent. There was a much-heard phrase in Alaska in those years—"Inside, Outside, Morningside."

We figured that Charlie put himself into Morningside trying to figure out how to win the ice pool.

For years we bought tickets on the Nenana Ice-pool, and twice came within minutes of winning.

That May Bud bought a 14-foot Aluma Craft boat and a 9-horsepower Evinrude outboard motor. While patiently waiting for the ice to go out of the Chena River, Bud frequently put his new toy—the Evinrude outboard—in a barrel of water, started it, and watched it churn the water. He loved it. After breakup we explored every river near Fairbanks, thoroughly enjoying our new mode of transportation.

Like Bud, I too had dreams of owning a dog team. I arrived home one day with what I thought was a real Siberian husky pup. Spookie was a recently-weaned, tiny, female. When she was grown I would breed her, and I'd raise the pups for my very own dog team. Knowing little of true sled dogs I was too pleased with my puppy to notice the sly smiles as I bragged about my future team. Spookie never grew to be very large, but she was well mannered and easily trained. But once I began to understand a little about sled dogs I no longer identified her as a Siberian husky, and I quit talking about her pups becoming a dog team.

I visited some people who raised and trained racing sled dogs and they gave me a six-week old male malemute that was the runt of the litter and so shy that he hid his head in a corner whenever anyone came near. I carried him home to Bud and announced "maybe-we-can-use-this-too," as if it was another piece of hardware. We became collectors of all sorts of things, looking ahead to building our lodge.

Bud became fond of the pup from the first, but he had no hope of it growing to be a work dog. He was wrong. Keno

Lenora tried hard to make the dogs go.

grew to be a strong sled dog and eventually the leader of our team. If Keno had a problem it was the fact that he was a one-man dog. He would follow and work his heart out for Bud, and he was a faithful pet all the years we had him. He was typical malemute, with a bit of white under his chin and belly, and two white dots over his warm brown eyes.

Bud brought home the three dogs he had purchased from Gareth Wright. Jim was a trained leader, too old to race any more. He was black with dots over his eyes. Black Boy was big, strong, and all-black. Wooley was white and wooley.

Every evening after work we built dog harness and rigged tow lines, and our living room was cluttered with rope, collars, straps, and tools. When we finally had harnesses that fit each dog, snow-time was too long a wait for Bud: he wanted to try out his dog team immediately. He repaired an old tin-bottomed toboggan someone had discarded, and decided to see if the dogs would pull that on the tall lush grass he had found on a side road near Fairbanks.

"We'll try 'em out to see if we have sled dogs, or just some expensive pets," he said as an excuse.

I drove the Jeep with the toboggan lashed to the top, with Jim and the two pups inside with me. Bud sat in the trailer holding the other two dogs. We had made such a pet of Jim that we feared he would want to ride the toboggan in preference to being lead dog.

All the dogs were excited and yipping as Bud harnessed them and hooked them to the tow line. He had made harnesses for the two pups too, since he figured they might just as well start learning. I held onto Jim's collar to keep him at the end of the towline because he wanted to see what was happening behind him, and also, I think, he wanted to jump up and lick Bud's face as he had been doing every chance when Bud stooped over.

"Jim, I may be just learning but I do know lead dogs are supposed to lean into their harness to keep the line tight while Bud harnesses the rest of the team!" I told the big dog. He ignored me until I cut a sturdy willow switch. He immediately lay quiet, and I went to help Bud with the other dogs. Both pups appeared bewildered and stood side-by-side ahead of the two wheel dogs (those nearest sled).

The toboggan was tied to a tree. When Bud was ready he told me to get aboard for the ride. He yanked the rope free and hollered, "Let's go!"

The dogs lunged ahead but the toboggan didn't move.

"I guess you're too heavy and they can't get started," Bud said, scratching his head. "Better get off."

I wasn't even clear of the toboggan and on my feet when those dogs were off with such a burst of speed that they pulled Bud off his feet and dragged him on his belly. He rolled at least two full turns from belly to back before he could slow them down and get to his feet. No telling where they'd have gone had he let loose of the tow rope.

The jackrabbit start had taken both pups by surprise, and they too had been dragged on their bellies and sides. Bud's shouts of "whoa" had no effect until the three had managed to run several hundred feet. I was laughing too hard to be of any assistance. Besides, they were going so fast I couldn't have caught them.

Both Bud and I were laughing so hard we could hardly hold the team for a second more coordinated try. This time I had a fast ride on the slippery grass after Bud persuaded leader Jim that LeNora was going to stay on the toboggan this time. He was convinced they had bluffed him once, but not for the second time. Keno took to pulling the toboggan like a veteran, for blood always tells, and Spookie did whatever Keno did, for she loved him dearly.

Bud was satisfied with the way the dogs worked in harness. When they tired that warm afternoon we crowded three dogs into the Jeep behind us and put the pups on the seat between us. The dogs in the rear weren't too tired to growl and start a fight when one or another crowded too much. Bud stopped the Jeep and settled dog fights twice on our way home. He'd have been chagrined had any of our dog-mushing friends seen us working our team on green grass. It worked though.

When we had been in Alaska a year we no longer considered ourselves cheechakos. We had survived Fairbanks' hottest summer and coldest winter in many a year. We had worked, explored, made friends, and settled down. We had started to serve our apprenticeship barely knowing what we were getting into. Now we knew without a doubt that Alaska was to be our home. There were times, I admit, when I thought longingly of the warmth and conveniences of California, but Alaska was like a magnet, and I wanted to see and do everything possible. Bud never swerved: he knew that Alaska was for him right from the start. Since we had burned our bridges, I really never gave serious thought to leaving.

That second summer every weekend and holiday found us scouting the country: we drove wherever the Jeep could go, and took our boat into rivers, streams, and lakes. Most of our travels were within a weekend drive of Fairbanks and our jobs. We decided to explore the Wrangell Mountains before we made a decision on where to build our lodge. We avidly studied every map of Alaska we could find, and read every book or article we could lay our hands on that gave us information that might help us choose our spot. Somehow the Wrangell Mountains fascinated us.

Our friends Joe and Lillian Heffron suggested we make a camping trip with them to the Tok Highway and Nabesna Road. Bud worked with Joe at Ladd Field. "We know you'll like that country," they predicted. Lillian was making jewelry with wild flowers, so our trip was a wildflower collecting trip for them. We planned the trip when all of us could take extra days from work plus our weekend, choosing a time in late August when the early autumn colors were at their best.

We loved the Nabesna Road from the start. Narrow, winding, and 40 miles long from the Tok Highway to the Nabesna mine, it lies in the heart of some of the finest scenery in North America—at the foot of the great Wrangell Mountains. We found a chain across the road at the Nabesna Mine, and the caretaker was gone. We'd have loved to explore around that old well-known but closed mine. There was a neat little cabin close to the road and near a two-story house where the mine caretaker lived, but no one was home. The cabin gave a breathtaking view of the mountains from the front porch. Obviously no one had lived in the cabin for a long time. We peeked in the win-

The trusty jeep.

Young musher driving his team.

dows, and I remarked to Bud that I'd love to spend a winter here if we could live in that cabin. Wishfull thinking.

But Bud promised he would locate the owner and ask about renting or using the cabin. He was excited about the vast area where perhaps he could trap, now that he had a dog team. It wasn't wishfull thinking on his part.

At Slana on the Tok Highway he learned that Bill Cameron, an Alaska Road Commission employee at Valdez, owned the cabin. Bill gave us permission to use the cabin for the coming winter for $60. Our intuition was that the Wrangell Mountains were right for us. Bud's assertiveness and decisive action to arrange for the cabin got our foot in the door, so to speak: now it was up to us to find the exact spot for our lodge, and to go on from there.

Before we left Fairbanks to move to Bill Cameron's cabin, Bud was to make a moose hunt in late September. He was now a resident, with a resident hunting license. He hunted with Roy Becker, a co-worker at Ladd Field who knew a place where there were always moose. Roy promised that Bud could shoot the first moose, he would shoot the second, and they would help each other pack the meat out.

Roy questioned Bud's choice of rifle—his trusty .30–30. He had used it for deer and other game in New Mexico and had great confidence in it. On his first moose hunt in Alaska Bud shot a moose with the .30–30, but the moose didn't drop as he expected it to. Instead it charged right toward him. Roy dropped the moose a few feet in front of Bud with his larger and more powerful .30–06 rifle.

Immediately after Bud and Roy returned to Fairbanks and had cared for their thousand pounds of moose meat, Bud headed for a gun shop and bought a Winchester Model 70 .30–06. It was the rifle he used for many years as a guide. We have it yet in Bud's trophy room.

# VI

## WE MOVE TO NABESNA

Charm, we called her, and the name fit the fuzzy black kitten from the early fall day I carried her home until she finally went the way of all pets some years later. She did seem to lead a charmed life, for she survived some cruel experiences—from the time I found her mewling unhappily, an abandoned or lost baby.

Bud was dubious about adding a cat to his dog-dominated household. There was also the incredibly long list of supplies and gear already packed and waiting to be loaded into our Jeep and trailer for the trip to Nabesna.

Both of us left good-paying jobs at Fairbanks to chase our dream of building a hunting lodge. We had even bought a log house at Fairbanks, making monthly payments on a mortgage. When I look back at ourselves I am astonished: we had little money, and few prospects of earning any. But we were young, optimistic, excited, and we were in a land that breeds success. In our minds there was no question but what we would succeed. And, of course, we were full of energy.

Son Lloyd drove a supply truck from Valdez to Fairbanks from late summer until mid-winter, and was then inducted into the Army and served his time at Fort Richardson near Anchorage.

In late August we had bid Fay goodbye as she boarded a plane at Fairbanks to fly back to San Diego to finish her high schooling there.

71

We left Fairbanks on October 30, 1948 with the trailer loaded and covered with a tarpaulin. The three Huskies and little black Spookie-dog were settled atop boxes loaded level like a floor behind the front seats where they lay side-by-side stretched out in order to have breathing room. Keno, the pup, was in his favorite place between us on the front seat. Charm was secure in her wooden box on my lap: the box was reinforced, since we feared the close-quarters excitement that would prevail if the cat was loosed with the sled dogs.

Charm's loud protests at being confined lasted all day, and all of the dog's ears were inquisitively pointed toward her box. Occasionally a dog emitted a low threatening growl aimed at a crowding companion, but a terse command from Bud usually settled the situation without fireworks.

We had groceries and camp gear with us and camped out, for we felt a bit too gamey with all the dog hair on our persons to present ourselves at any respectable roadhouse. Also, if we had chosen to remain overnight at a roadhouse we knew that Keno would wail continuously as he always did when out of Bud's sight. Guests trying to sleep wouldn't appreciate his music.

All went well until late evening when we camped in an old shelter cabin beside the highway. The dogs were tied to nearby trees, but I worried that the cat would wander away in the strange surroundings. I lifted a loose floor board of the cabin and set her on the dry ground underneath, trusting she would come back into the room when she finished. Instead she found a small hole and squeezed herself through to investigate what lay behind the walls of the cabin. Jim had slipped his collar, and Bud had left Keno untied as he never ventured far from Bud's person. The two dogs seeing the cat emerge from under the cabin lay in wait until she was far beyond easy retreat, then they pounced. That moment was nearly her exit from life.

At that opportune moment I opened the door to toss out the dishwater. As I did a furry black cat hurtled past me as though she had been catapulted from space. Her tail was twice normal size, and her eyes blazed defiance. She turned

72

in mid-air and with scratching claws raked both dogs' noses as they rushed headlong through the door behind her. Between the cat's scratches and Bud's cussing, the dog's egos were suddenly deflated. They departed with drooping tails and made themselves scarce for the balance of the evening. After this incident they showed a marked respect for Charm.

We reached Slana, located near the start of the Nabesna Road, near dark on that short October day, and had dinner at Duffy's Tavern and store, a three-story log building and a landmark roadhouse. It also happened to be the post office. We introduced ourselves to owners Don and Zazz Duffy and their son Don Jr. We would come to know the Duffy's as friends in the coming years.

Eager to get settled in our new home, despite the frosting of windshield and side windows from so much dog, people, and cat breath, we drove the long slow winding 40 miles of the Nabesna Road, while peering through a tiny opening in the windshield. It was late in the evening when finally we reached our lovely little log cabin. The dogs came first. Each was tied to one of the dog houses already there. Then they were fed. While every dog busily sniffed and investigated every inch of its new home, Bud set up our little Yukon stove inside the cabin and got a fire going in it. I soon had tea water boiling and was busily packing in the groceries and cooking pots and pans and establishing my kitchen. The aroma of bacon and potatoes and onions frying, and the fragrant odor of wood smoke hastened Bud as he unpacked the Jeep. Satiated with food, tired from the long drive, relaxed in the warm cabin after the cold October air, we made the bed in eager anticipation of a comfortable night's sleep.

I was up with the sun and had a fire going and the coffee perking when the neighbor from the two-story log house less than a city block away knocked at our door. He was Harry Boyden, a legendary Alaskan, a genuine sourdough who was a noted packer for big game outfitters with his packstring of horses. He sometimes guided on these hunts, but mostly he furnished the horses and handled them as a full-time job. He handled up to 30 horses. In his day, guided

Bud hauling supplies by dog team.

hunts were made almost entirely with horses, and most hunts lasted at least 30 days. Born in England, he came to Alaska when he was 18, and still retained a broad accent. He had a bucket of water in one hand and an armload of wood in the other—his way of welcoming us to our new home. Harry had gracious manners, and seemed pleased that we had arrived. For many winters previous he had been the sole resident of Nabesna. In his sixties, he had retired from packing and guiding, and was the caretaker for the long-closed Nabesna gold mine.

Within two days we had everything put away and had set up housekeeping in our new home in the wilderness. The cabin had three rooms, with a window in the living room looking out at Devil's Mountain, one of the prominent sub-peaks of the great Wrangell range. Actually, every window of the cabin was a frame for magnificent high peaks that stretched into the deep blue Alaskan sky. There were neat cupboards in the kitchen and a little bedroom with a clothes closet. The living room had a smooth board floor, and a smooth finished floor is seldom found in cabins built far from the city. Bill Cameron had brought his bride to that cabin when he was a timekeeper at the then-operating Nabesna Mine. Even the garage (an unusual feature in a wilderness cabin) was well constructed and had a sturdy smooth floor.

I moved the kitchen table into the front room by the big window where we could eat and look across to the snow-covered peaks and watch the constantly changing scenes as the morning sun slowly changed from rose to brilliant sunlight. I spent many satisfying hours by this window writing or reading when Bud was away on the trap line.

Charm covered every inch of the cabin, thoroughly sniffing and inspecting all articles and corners. Finding everything satisfactory to her feline taste, she made herself at home on a high shelf in a corner where, with watchful eyes, she could survey the activities of her human companions. Her black form was difficult to see; often only her huge yellow eyes gave a clue to her whereabouts, and she passed many contented hours on that shelf that winter. We soon discovered that the kitchen table was beyond her vision, and any rattle of dishes from that sector was sure to bring a thud as she leaped to the floor and bounded out with a hopeful meooow, expecting a handout. She didn't seem to realize how many times we waited until she was comfortably settled on her lofty perch and then deliberately rattled a dish on the table to bring her running. She never failed us a laugh at her expense; perhaps she also enjoyed the game.

Winter was near, and we had to have a supply of firewood for the kitchen range and airtight heater. With the Jeep and trailer and a road to travel on, it was a fairly simple project. The two pups, Keno and Spookie, always went along to romp and chase while I sat by a cozy fragrant sprucewood fire while Bud did the sawing. I helped carry the pieces to the trailer.

Harry Boydon came to inspect the wood and complimented Bud on knowing good dry wood. Birch and green woods have a tendency to burn too hot, or to soot a chimney too fast. Bud slyly grinned, for he didn't regard himself as a cheechako in the woods.

Every evening for a while the dog harnesses were spread on the front room floor for modification and further finishing in readiness for the coming winter. Boyden had mushed many a dog team, and we welcomed his occasional suggestions about the dogs, the harness, and the sled. He pointed out a wrong connection on the harness, and a snap that wouldn't stand the strain when the dogs were pulling a heavy load. This piece was too short or too long, and that collar would fit this dog better—see how his neck is different? Experience tells.

By November 12th we had a fair pile of wood stacked near the cabin, neatly sawed up to fit the stoves. The Jeep had a power take-off, and Bud had acquired a buzz saw. Boyden helped Bud with ours, then Bud helped him with his wood.

On the long winter evenings when the men came into the house hungry I did enjoy cutting a fresh-baked pie and serving coffee. Each time Harry sat with us even for a short time he had a new story to tell. Bud and I listened intently.

The temperature dropped to zero by November 16, and on that day Bud and I accompanied Boyden on the six mile walk to the Nabesna River bar where he wanted to pull the shoes off of his pack horses. Harry had a nice little cabin and a corral there for his horses. We were surprised to see such fat glossy-coated horses that came from where they had been grazing along the river when Harry yelled for them. Each horse had its turn at poking its nose into the oat bag Harry held. Each horse was patted and stroked and called by name. Seven of them were old, but didn't look it— one was even 30, quite old for a horse. Harry used them only in the fall hunting season, and they were fed grain during the coldest winter months. It was a pleasure to see a man treat his animals with so much concern and thoughtful care.

Harry explained that his horses had been faithful workers all the years he had owned them. They had traveled many a trail with him, and had patiently carried packs of all kinds under all conditions while out with his hunting parties. With pawing through the deep snow and cold in winter hunting their own grub, fighting mosquitoes and other insects in summer, Harry said that any little kindness he could show them was no more than they had earned.

We saw signs of the old road where during World War II freight had been trucked from Valdez. From a big gravel airfield at Nabesna bush planes had hauled tons of freight, including tar for paving, to Northway for the airport built there. The Northway Airport was one of a string of airports used by warplanes flown from the U.S. to Fairbanks, thence to Nome and on to Russia where these lend lease planes fought the Nazis.

Snow finally arrived at Nabesna on November 18, when the white stuff came down all day and all night, turning the world into a winter wonderland. Harry harnessed his dog team and drove it down the road past our house while I helped Bud harness our team. Soon Bud drove our team in Boyden's trail, with the two untrained pups having a glorious time barking and running along. Neither knew enough to pull, so their tug lines were slack. Jim kept them moving ahead, and occasionally he pulled one or the other off of its feet. All of the dogs were too fat, and they needed to be toughened for the trap line trails. Charm sat in the

Waiting for spring and open water.

window watching as Bud and the team arrived back in the yard two hours later. I went out to help unhook and tie the dogs to their houses. The dog feed was cooked and cooled, and I helped Bud feed them before he came in for hot tea after shedding his heavy clothing. He then told me of the two hour run with the dogs, and how each dog behaved.

After that Bud and Harry ran their teams down the road and back twice each day. The men and the dogs enjoyed this activity like kids with new sleds. Each day they went a mile farther before turning back. At first they went five miles, and soon ten miles a day as the dogs toughened. Keno and Spookie learned to pull and keep running forward instead of forever peering back. Jim knew when they slacked off and he yanked them forward.

A week before Thanksgiving Bud thought the dogs were tough enough for a four day trip. He wanted to set up a tent and get ready for trapping. He had trail to break for the last few miles to the site he had chosen for the tent.

The 6×8 tent with 3-foot sidewalls, the small Yukon stove, bedroll, grub box, dog feed, and traps made a heavy load. Charm and I stood in the window as Bud harnessed the dogs, a show I never tired of. Jim stood at the end of his tow rope barking, looking back every minute or so to see what was taking so long. Little black Spookie was next in harness and hooked to the tow line. She stood with tail between her legs until Keno was in harness beside her, then she wiggled and barked as if to say everything was ok now that Keno was there. Wooley had a loud persistent yap, still tied to his house, reminding Bud not to forget him. Black Boy did his share of excited barking to be sure to let Bud know he wanted to get going. He lunged into his harness to test if the sled was still tied. As the last dog was hooked up, Jim came back and licked Bud in the face as he leaned over. He was picked up bodily and deposited back at the end of his line and commanded in stern tones, "Stay there."

Finally Bud yanked loose the tie rope holding the sled to a tree, grabbed the handlebars, and in an instant the dogs lunged forward and sprinted down the trail at full speed. Bud barely had time for a farewell wave before they were out of sight around the bend.

Charm knew the excited barking of the dogs when they were being harnessed for a trip, and she was an interested spectator for the entire proceeding, watching from the large front window until dogs and driver were out of sight around a bend. Then with an obviously satisfied "purrrt" she jumped to the floor and came running to curl in my lap or to sit close to where I was working to tell me how happy she was that they were gone, and that she hoped they would stay away a few days so she could sleep with me rather than sleep alone in her box in the shed.

Long before I heard a sound, without fail Charm heard the dogs and Bud returning and ran to her window lookout. There she remained until the last dog was unharnessed and led away to be tied at its house.

My black kitty was fine company when Bud and the dogs were gone. I kept myself busy in many ways. I tried hard to make a batch of yeast bread that was as good as that of Harry Boyden's. We greatly admired his skill as a baker, and he frequently brought us a loaf of his golden brown bread. I read my cookbooks, learning to cook wild meats, and learning to do without many things because the grocery store was so far away. While Bud was gone I sewed a set of red curtains for the windows, and made pretty little red flowers from pieces of felt.

It turned warm and the snow on the roof melted. On my first evening alone I was quietly writing when a large hunk of snow let loose from the roof with a resounding crash. I jumped, but the cat jumped higher, tail fuzzed twice normal size as she ran for cover. When we were both adjusted to the quiet again, another chunk slid off the roof as unexpectedly and just as loud as the first. Startled again, I wondered if being alone was going to be so great after all. I turned the battery radio on for company, and amazingly, picked up a New Mexico station that advertised flower bulbs that would bloom into beautiful flowers anywhere. Alaska, I wondered? I drifted into a dream world, remembering San Diego and my rose garden and gardenias, thinking that the poinsettias would soon be blooming. I looked out the window and the snowy scene brought me back to reality.

I learned to light the Coleman lantern, and became profi-

Trouble on the freight run.

cient in building fires in our kitchen range in the airtight space heater. I was proud of myself for being able to quickly lose my city ways, and to not have to depend on Bud to do everything.

Time flew, and just at dark on the third day that Bud and the dogs had been gone Charm leaped to the window sill, tail fuzzed, and gave a warning "meow." The dogs soon appeared around the bend, all frosty-faced, red tongues hanging, as they trotted tiredly. Bud's parka ruff was all frosted from his breath. The wind had blown a gale all morning, blasting the snow off the trees, and Bud and the dogs had had to face into it all the way home. The dogs were clearly happy to get home and in their houses out of the wind. With full bellies they curled up, tails over noses, with no wailing choruses. Keno and Spookie scratched at the door for permission to come in and curl up by the fire for a while, after begging a handout. Then they were content to snuggle in their own houses. Bud was tired too, and appreciated the fact that I had cooked the dog feed. He had set out traps and wanted to return home rather than spend another night in the tent.

On Thanksgiving 1948 we had a wonderful dinner and two guests. Harry cooked a big moose roast that was moist, tender, and delicious. He also loaned Bud an ice cream freezer. I made pies and cooked a variety of vegetables, and Smoke Thomas, who a week early had moved into the cabin by Skookum Creek down the road a ways, brought wild cranberry Jell-o. We played pinochle until the evening news came on, and then listened to Tundra Topics, the messages to bush residents from KFAR, Fairbanks.

That winter we spent many pleasant evenings playing cards at our cabin or Harry's. At Harry's we often looked at his the picture albums of hunting trips, and autographed books from hunters he had taken on hunts. Sometimes we simply enjoyed being entertained by his wonderful stories. His library fascinated me; all fine books, and he had read them all.

## VII

## BUD'S TRAP LINE

By late November 1948 Bud's dog team trips to check his trap line had become routine. The trail he followed was well packed and solid, and the dogs were toughened enough so he could leave the cabin at 7 a.m. and be home in time for dinner. He got used to returning against the wind on icy windy days. Once he returned with a frosted Adam's apple, and nipped fingers, making it difficult for him to skin the animals he caught. On some trips he found nothing in his traps; others as few as two animals. I pretended I knew nothing about skinning animals, for that was one part of being a trapper's wife where I was reluctant. There were times I felt I should have helped and that I could have learned, but instead I learned to knit wool socks for him instead.

I accompanied Bud and the dogs on short trips. Sometimes I would ride out with them for a few miles and walk back to the cabin while Bud went on. I was getting myself in condition for running behind the sled, for the dogs seldom allowed me to ride the runners for long. When they were on an easy trail or going downhill it was all right, otherwise they would stop and look back, sending me the clear message to get off.

Bud talked me into going with him to his tent where we were to remain overnight. The weather was simply too inviting that day for me to refuse. I was well aware of his endurance on the trail, and I questioned my physical ability to handle such a long trip, but he assured me it was an easy trail, and that I could ride a lot. I hesitated until he put in extra grub, a plate and cup in the grub box, and tied my sleeping bag in the sled. The temperature was plus 20 degrees F., without a breath of wind.

While I got into my winter clothing Charm rubbed against my legs, letting me know she wanted to go too. I told her not this time. Usually we took her in her sturdy box tied on the sled, but it hurt the Huskies' dignity to have to pull a sled with a cat aboard. Only Keno tolerated the cat and protected her from the other dogs. She knew enough to keep her distance from the sled dogs, and she knew the exact length of their chains. She also knew I was leaving her when I carried her to the garage with enough moose meat and water to last, then closed the door.

The dogs were always eager to run, and they took off at a face pace with me in the bouncing sled, with Bud on the runners. Bud used the brake going down the first steep hill and the babiche holding the brake on the sled broke when the claw caught on a rock. The long brake board sprang back, barely missing hitting him in the face. Sled dogs, especially a leader, know when they have an advantage, and Jim was no exception. He ran faster when he realized the sled had no brake, and it was quite a ways before Bud's "Whoa, Jim," stopped the team. It helped when he used a few auxiliary words that they recognized—words that erupted when they had pushed him as far as they dared without retribution.

There was no handy tree to tie the sled rope to so I held onto Jim, who was eager to get going, while Bud repaired the brake with babiche he always carried. When we got under way I had a long walk up a steep hill and across a creek. The sled was heavy, and the dogs knew Bud would help by pushing, so they stopped and looked back when the pulling became hard.

We both rode down the next hill. We had gone ten miles and it seemed to me that it had been mostly uphill. I was tired and I thought that maybe we'd get to the tent soon, but the trail turned from the road and headed three miles across hummocky tundra. Even with the well-packed broken trail

I couldn't ride the sled, for it fell off the trail on one side or the other whenever I did. Bud would push it back on, and the dogs could keep moving. I stumbled along behind them, and all too frequently the crusted snow gave way beneath my feet, and I plunged through with one foot. I got so angry a few times that I simply sat there until I got cold, then I got up and went on until I caught up to where the team was waiting at the top of a rise.

"Ride the runners and balance the sled by leaning," Bud urged, but I couldn't hold the sled on the trail with its heavy load, and the dogs simply stopped every time it left the trail. Then I had to wait for Bud to get it back on the trail. The dogs wouldn't budge to help me pull it back. However the instant Bud touched the handles they pulled fiercely. It was all very frustrating.

I rode when the trail crossed frozen pothole lakes, but there weren't many of them. By the time I staggered into the tent I was tuckered out, anyway clearly not tough enough to mush that dog team on that trail. Bud got a fire going in the little stove with dog feed cooking, and I propped myself up with my sleeping bag behind me, sitting on Bud's, and the blessed warmth in the tent soon put me to sleep. Bud woke me when dinner was ready.

I crawled into my sleeping bag after eating, and was oblivious until Bud called me in the morning for the return trip home. Going back wasn't nearly so bad. The day was mild and sunny, and I enjoyed being out in the silent woods. Charm was so happy to have me home that she rubbed against my legs and sat on my lap talking all evening.

For much of November and into late December Bud was home for three days or so, then he would leave with the dogs for two or three days and stay at the tent to check his traps. He and the dogs became toughened to the trail, and they came home less tired each time. On the days he arrived home, after a hot meal he would describe for me the events of his trip. Then he would go out to the garage and build a fire in the stove and skin the animals he had caught. Occasionally he skinned a small animal in the front room, for it saved on wood, and we could talk while he was working, or he could listen to the radio. I was not adjusted to seeing the animals he brought in that were caught in traps. I felt sad for them, but I realized I was married to a man who planned to supplement our income by trapping and selling the furs.

There was only the small Yukon stove in the tent, and he cooked the dog feed first in the evening before warming the stew I cooked for him. The little stove didn't stay warm very long without wood, so he had to get up frequently during the night to build up the fire. It started getting very cold in December, and during one night when he slept in the tent the temperature dropped to $-40$ F. That's cold, and it's hard on man and dog to be out in it.

I cooked dog feed when Bud was out with the team, but I hated the smell from the dried salmon in it. We cooked it out of doors when the wind wasn't blowing, or when it wasn't real cold. When I had to cook it in the house I sat quite still in a corner and managed to ignore the smell until the corn meal was cooked and it could be carried out, and then I opened the door to let fresh air in.

Hard working sled dogs need a quarter of a pound of tallow each every day, cooked with the cornmeal and fish. It keeps their coats conditioned to deep winter cold and provides them with energy. Later someone told me that the dried fish could be put into the hot cornmeal after the cooked food was taken from the stove and set out to cool. Now why didn't I think of that?

On December 20 we received word that the cornmeal (for dog food) we had ordered and expected for weeks had arrived at Duffy's. Bud left next morning with the Jeep for the 40 mile drive to Slana. We needed other supplies, as well as mail. The temperature was $-35$ degrees F. when he left, but Bud decided to go anyway because the Nabesna Road was not maintained in winter, and drifting snow usually closed it until spring. We expected this to be the last trip with the Jeep for the winter.

Bud had no difficulty on the drive to Slana. Once there he didn't dare shut the engine off for fear he couldn't restart it. He ran errands, but didn't delay. With a grin he told me a number of folks had asked, "How's LeNora adjusting?"

During the day the temperature dropped to $-40$ degrees F., and the fuel line of the Jeep froze up twice as Bud drove the lonely 40 miles home. He had no alcohol to put in the fuel tank to absorb the moisture. He built a fire to keep himself warm by, and then he removed the fuel line, melted the ice out of it, and also melted the ice out of the carburetor. He had all those little fittings to loosen and put back together with freezing fingers at −40! I don't know how he did it. Twice he went through this routine, and twice he restarted the Jeep and drove on. He was chilled to the bone when he arrived home, for the cab of the Jeep had canvas sides, and the heat escaped almost as fast as the heater provided it.

Mail again, the first in a month. I could hardly wait to open letters and pour through them before getting Bud something hot to eat and drink. What excitement for a gal who was used to having mail delivered to her door in San Diego!

For Christmas that year I had a fat and pretty little spruce tree that we cut in the nearby woods. I had no conventional tree ornaments, but I decorated it with tinsel cut from strips of our cigarette packages. I made red poinsettias from old scraps of felt I found on a shelf, and I had an ample supply of green wrapping paper for leaves and to wrap the stems. As I worked on these I could picture poinsettias red and beautiful against my white stucco California home. I was almost homesick, as this was to be a time away from home and my kids again.

On Christmas eve Harry Boyden brought three small packages wrapped in colorful paper and tied with bright red string and hung them on our tree. I made a gold star from the inside of envelopes from two Christmas cards. I had strings of popcorn on the tree, and little Santas, their beards made from the cotton left from the old mattress someone had once caulked the cabin with. Little fluffs of the same cotton dotting the tree here and there made us an attractive tree.

Harry was to play Santa Claus, and we waited all Christmas morning for him. He was also to have eaten breakfast with us, but didn't show, although he was usually very punctual. We had played pinochle with him until the previous midnight, so figured he might have been sleeping.

Horsetail Falls in Thompson Pass.

Like kids, we were excited and wanted to see what was in the three little packages Harry had hung on our tree. We also were excited about opening other packages, including some from home.

Finally at one o'clock we could stand it no longer and walked to Harry's to see what was delaying him. He was washing clothes! He had decided to take a bath and put on clean clothes for the holiday. After carrying and heating bath water he didn't want to waste it, so he washed his clothes in it. Then, by golly, he still didn't want to throw all the nice warm water out, so he scrubbed his floor with it. We wished him a Merry Christmas, and he promised he'd be along soon. There was no rushing him, I learned.

Finally at two o'clock here came Harry, greeting us with a hearty "Ho Ho, Merry Christmas." He was nonchalant about being late for our Christmas party. Our folks had sent a variety of interesting and unusual items in their Christmas packages. Bud's mother had sent a care package that included toilet paper. We made highballs from the three little bottles of whiskey Harry had hung from our tree—one for each of us. Harry had collected them during a commercial airline flight to the east coast when he went to a dinner for the Webb family that he had guided on a big game hunt one year. He had saved them several years for this very special occasion.

Our Christmas dinner was roasted ptarmigan with wild cranberry sauce, plus pies and the usual wide variety of vegetables. I decorated the table with paper Santa Clauses. After dinner we listened to the news while eating ice cream Bud had made to go with the pie. The radio went dead, and we discovered that a tube had blown. We hadn't thought to bring extras. For the rest of the winter our Philco battery radio was simply a nice ornament.

On the day after Christmas Bud left before daylight with the dogs to check traps. The dogs were eager to be on the trail after their rest. Bud later told me that Jim had decided to turn down the wrong trail at the Nabesna Bar, rather than go where Bud wanted to go. After a stop and a short argument, Jim led out again, this time going where Bud wanted to go.

I hurried to get the washing done. It took a long time to melt enough snow for both washing and rinsing, bring enough wood in for the day, and to bake bread. Harry came over in the afternoon and we played rummy. I won all three games, and he wryly said he was going to kick his dog Pal all the way home because he hadn't won even one game.

The wind came up and was blowing almost a blizzard on the day I expected Bud to come home. I kept thinking about him and I was uneasy about him traveling in such weather. I looked out the window frequently all that short dark day. It was almost dark when Charm leaped up in the big front window and said "Murrrt" to alert me that Bud and the team was coming. I heard a "Gee, Jim," and as I looked out I saw the dogs lying quietly in their traces, their breath forming frost on their muzzles. Bud's parka ruff was frosted, and he looked like an Eskimo. The knee was out of his pant leg, ripped from the brush. He was limping. I went out to help unharness the dogs and hooked them to their chains at their houses.

The weather was very cold for his entire trip, and he had frozen a big toe while setting traps. He knew his foot was cold at the time, but he hadn't investigated. A seam had ripped in the moosehide moccasins he wore, and snow had packed inside it. I had dog feed cooked, so we fed the tired animals immediately, and they gratefully bedded down for well-deserved rest. After dinner Bud soaked his swollen and painful foot in hot water filled with Epsom salts. I gave him three aspirins and he slept soundly the night through. For two days he hobbled around the cabin and yelled if I ventured anywhere near his propped-up foot.

On the last day of the year the temperature climbed from −30 degrees F. to well above zero, but the wind blew so strongly that it felt much colder. Bud left with the dog team long before daylight to check his traps, and was home much earlier than I expected, absolutely elated. He had caught the wolverine that had been springing some of his traps. He had seen its tracks on his trail on his last three times out. He spent the evening skinning the 35-pound animal. It's fur was glossy and thick, a lovely skin.

Charm loved to ride on my shoulder when I went out-

90

Loading up the Super Cub.

doors. One day I missed her, and wondered where in the world she could be. Some red squirrels were creating a greater disturbance than usual, and I went to see what they were hollering about. I found that I had locked Charm in the outhouse—and she had been there since morning. She was indignant.

Keno and Spookie-dog were seldom tied, and they had accepted the cat as part of the household. They ignored her as she went about her own interests out of doors, or when they were allowed in the cabin to lie for a few minutes on the rug by the fire. The cat was mistress of the house, and always watchfully and arrogantly eyed them from the back of the high leather chair.

When she wanted out, there were plenty of tall trees close at hand, so even when the dog team was at leisure I allowed her out, feeling she was capable of taking care of herself.

One day I glanced out of the window in time to see the cat furiously dash past, heading in the direction of the front porch with three bounding dogs uncomfortably close to her fuzzed-out tail. I ran out in time to see Charm leap to the window sill. Smart little Spookie caught her tail just as her feet struck the window ledge, and yanked the poor cat back amidst the snapping dogs. I simultaneously landed atop the whole mass of squirming dogs and cat, cussing and threatening the dogs. Somehow Charm maneuvered herself free, and when I extricated myself and gained my feet I saw her meowing forlornly from the thick branches of a nearby tall tree. The dogs, who were no fools, chagrined at missing the cat, looked sheepishly at their disheveled mistress, then at the treed cat, then made a fast retreat into the woods beyond my reach.

Jim had managed to slip his choke collar and he had excited the other two dogs enough so they joined him in the chase. It could easily have been Charm's exit from this life. I noticed soon after that she wised up to another ploy of the dogs. Their teamwork was astounding to me as I watched an abortive effort to trap her; a loose dog lay close to his house, pretending he was tied, while two other loose dogs positioned themselves close to the trees, ready to cut her off if she suckered and moved within striking distance of the "loose" dog. On another occasion I watched Charm and one of the dogs use the same tactics in trying to nail a squirrel that was teasing them.

As 1948 ended we could look back on our accomplishments: surviving in our wilderness cabin, developing our dog team, establishing a trap line and trapping fur, coping with the wind and the deep cold.

Next was to be our trial by snow.

## VIII

## SNOW

On New Year's day 1949 Bud and I walked over to Harry Boyden's to listen to the Rosebowl football game on his radio. Bud hobbled on a badly swollen foot. When we returned home he made ice cream, and that foot stuck out awkwardly and he yelled if either Harry or I ventured close: it was tender.

Smoke Thomas, our other neighbor, left to go to another area to trap, and I missed the evening chorus of the three dog teams. First Smoke's dogs would sing a high note, and ours would join in. Then Harry's seven dogs would start singing. Some of the dogs had their own style of wailing, and I could pick out individuals that had unique notes. A city girl, enjoying the singing of northern sled dogs? My values and interests had certainly changed since moving to Alaska.

After dinner and dessert New Year's eve, Bud, Harry, and I played many games of pinochle. Competition was so keen that we stayed up much later than planned—far after midnight. Harry had planned to leave for Slana for mail and supplies early in the morning, but decided to wait a day or two in order to catch up on his rest before attempting the long dog team trip.

Harry ran seven well-trained dogs, and it was a pleasure to see him handle them. My amusement was evident while I watched him carefully getting ready for his trip to Slana and packing a roll of paper money and lots of mail in what he

Cleaning fish for dinner.

After dinner at Tanada Lake, a time for visiting.

referred to as "my expensive brief case"—a dingy well-used flour sack.

Bud and I planned to leave in a couple of days, but first he had to check his traps and leave them sprung for he expected to be gone for some time. I was supposed to have returned to Fairbanks and my drapery shop by this time: I had left an employee running it for me. I was worried about it.

Harry was gone before daylight on January third, and Bud took his dog team to check traps closest to home. The dogs were full of pep after the long rest, and Bud tried to hold them back on a long downhill run when he stubbed his sore toe as the sled tipped over on a curve. Despite the pain he hung onto the sled until he could stop the dogs. He removed his moosehide moccasin to find that a blister had broken, and the toe felt better. After another hot soaking in Epsom salts we thought the toe would survive. To protect it, Bud put a tin can over it inside his sock on his next trip.

We postponed leaving because the temperature had dropped to −22 F. and Bud's frozen toe was still aching. It was a 40 mile trip to Slana and the Tok Highway. Snow had drifted across the Nabesna Road, and it had been closed to wheeled traffic since Bud's trip out in November. While waiting we made fudge and popcorn, and I read aloud for a time. Then we played rummy, but we missed Harry, our pinochle partner. We also missed the radio. We had frequently listened to Harry's since the tube had burned out in ours. We were running low on Blazo for the Coleman lantern, so we delayed lighting the lantern as long as we could evenings.

Finally, Bud's frozen toe was back almost to normal. Then, of all things, he got a very large and long sliver from under our wooden table as he leaped to break up a dog fight. The sliver penetrated deep into the flesh just above his knee. He dug it out with the point of his knife, assuring me it was no big deal. But it did end up being a big deal. He got blood poisoning in the leg. All the Epsom salts poultices and everything else we could think of to try on it when it became puffy, red and purple and angry looking in a couple of days didn't help at all. A three-day blizzard kept us indoors while we doctored Bud's leg.

About then Jack John Justin, an Indian who lived at the three-family Indian village on the Nabesna bar about six miles away, arrived driving his dog team to see how we were getting along. He looked at Bud's leg and said to put a raw moose meat poultice on it and keep it on until the redness was gone. Gee! Should we try that? We had tried everything else, so we gave it a go, and it worked, and we soon had Bud ready for the trail again.

Another three-day storm kept us close to the cabin, again delaying our departure. We awoke on the morning of the ninth. It had snowed all night, and snow was still falling. We had planned to leave this day—again. The trail was covered with fresh snow and it was too deep for the dogs to travel. We amused ourselves with inside tasks, mending, and reading. Bud went out on snowshoes and cut down a dead tree and sawed it into firewood.

On the following day we awoke just as the sun was casting pencil lines of rose velvet across the white peaks, and found ourselves in a still-white world buried under four feet of light fluffy snow. Temperature was five degrees above zero. An hour later all the clouds had turned to shades of pink and deep rose. A dazzling panorama of sparkling whiteness and pearly gray made our little world a fairyland indeed. By noon the temperature had climbed to 18 above zero, the sun was shining bright, and not a breath of wind stirred the air. All the trees held their burdens of snow-covered branches like eternal sentries in a sleeping world. The white grandeur of the lofty peaks far above us sparkled in the sun—no goddess ever wore her white robes with more elegance.

Travel was impossible in that deep soft snow, so we postponed our departure for another day. We were impatient and restless, and the mild weather and beauty lured us out. The woods beyond our cabin were so inviting with the white-mantled trees that we put on snowshoes and hiked perhaps five miles up an old dry creek bed to the foot of a high stony peak, skirting thick timber on our return home.

Newly returned home, we were famished, and I was frying some juicy fat moose steaks, our mouths watering from the aroma, when our dogs set up a terrific racket. Bud grabbed his rifle and went to see what the fuss was all about. He found fresh wolf tracks in the nearby trees. The wolves were gone, but when he returned to the house he kept the rifle handy in event they returned. They didn't. Apparently they had been passing by and had come close enough to disturb the dogs. After dinner, with the dogs fed, he sat outside waiting in case they returned. I sat with no light, eagerly awaiting a rifle shot. Kitty came to sit in my lap, and my imagination worked overtime as I pictured the savage beasts slinking on padded feet through the dark trees, silently creeping up and grabbing Bud from behind. Just then a large chunk of snow slide from the roof with a crash. I jumped straight out of the chair, and Kitty went streaking across the floor and behind the stove, her tail three times normal size. I was thankful when Bud came in soon after.

Old Chief John from Nabesna Village had come one December afternoon bringing the front quarter of a moose he had just killed. He was out of sugar and tea, so I shared from what I thought was a generous supply. I had always lived where we could go to a store and buy whatever we were out of, so I underestimated what we would use. By the time we left the cabin that January we were almost out of tea, and we were out of sugar. And shortly I was out of baking powder.

When Jack John Justin stopped to visit I'm sure he chuckled to himself at my flat pancakes. He didn't tell me how to make sourdough. He assumed everyone knew that. I didn't. It was a long time later that I learned that simple recipe, and then I scolded Jack for not telling a dumb cheechako gal. He laughed. "You didn't ask," he said.

On January 11 we finally put kitty in her box and anchored it to the sled and started out for 40-mile-distant Slana. It was still snowing, and even with Bud going ahead and breaking trail with snowshoes, the trail was so soft and the snow so deep that it was hard going. We returned home.

Next day Bud left with the dog team to try to break trail to nine-mile-distant Jack Creek. It was almost six o'clock in the evening before he returned with the tired dogs. He hadn't been able to break more than six miles of trail. Bud snowshoed ahead with the dogs following until the sled ran off the trail into deep snow. The dogs would sit and howl until he returned and lifted the sled onto the trail again.

It snowed another three inches during the night, and still there was no wind to harden and crust the snow. The sky was clear with the temperature at 18 above. Again Bud took to the trail to keep what he had broken open, and to try to break trail farther. He reached the Jack Creek bridge, making about nine miles of broken trail. Bud and the dogs returned after six, and I fried ptarmigan for Bud's dinner, and had cooked a large pot of feed with double helpings for each dog. The kennels were unusually quiet that night, without the usual singing and occasional barks; the dogs were worn out from breaking trail.

Harry had been gone for a week, and we wondered if he was still at the settlement, or if he had started back on the trail home and couldn't make it. Perhaps he was at the tent at 17 mile, or Twin Lakes Cabin. Maybe he was at Rufus Creek with the Thompsons, but he would be hauling supplies back with him, so we didn't worry about him being out of grub.

Bud decided that if I went with him I could mush the dogs while he went ahead to break trail. We could take enough grub for two days, and we should at least get as far as Twin Lakes cabin. Also, while on the trail, I could hold the sled back so that Jim wouldn't hitchhike on the tails of Bud's snowshoes and keep tripping him—an exceedingly annoying habit.

But we had to wait, for another storm hit, and it was terribly cold and windy next morning. Bud and the dogs were still trail weary, so we waited for a couple of days. On the morning we were finally ready to start again, the sun broke over the snow-capped peaks, turning our white world to rose-tinted beauty with the temperature at ten above and not a breath of air stirring in the silent world. We loaded the sled heavily with supplies to last a few days—dog food and cooking pans, sleeping bags, food for ourselves and what we could spare to leave there for the long trip to Slana.

We found the trail that Bud had broken was drifted over

in most places, but it was solid underneath. Jim could follow the faint outline of the trail without difficulty. I went ahead on snowshoes most of the distance to Jack Creek, for Bud had trouble keeping the sled on the trail, and he had to help the dogs pull on most of the hills.

Before our next try Bud lashed a gee pole—a handle that projects ahead—to the sled, and we had to learn how to use it. The gee pole's length gives leverage, and it is used to help steer the sled to keep it on the trail. Sometimes a musher will wear skis and straddle the towline while hanging onto the gee pole and steering a sled. We didn't have skis, but hiked along in front of the sled and when necessary Bud threw his weight onto the gee pole, keeping the sled headed in the right direction.

That first day the sun was behind dark clouds long before we neared Jack Creek, and a cold breeze had sprung up. Luckily it was at our back. Still it chilled us when we stopped to rest. It was dreary and miserable on the trail, discouraging to Bud to have the trail he had broken with so much hard work drifted over again with fine loose snow. I was so exhausted by the time we neared a heavily timbered thicket that I insisted we stop and build a fire and make hot tea. I just knew that I couldn't keep going without tea. It was near dark, and Bud built a roaring fire, but by then the wind was blowing so hard that the flames lay level across the snow, and try as we would to huddle near, we just couldn't stay warm in front and back at the same time.

We felt much better after hot tea and a short rest, and we debated about turning back for home. We had to do something, and quickly, or we were going to freeze to death, for the icy wind knifed through our clothing. Bud worried about the five miles or so of unbroken trail ahead. I dreaded facing the icy wind all the way home, and preferred continuing on to the Twin Lakes cabin three miles farther on, even if it took far into the night, and if it meant stopping frequently to build fires.

I had forgotten my dark glasses and watch and had a headache from the bright sun reflecting from the snow. We judged the moon would come up around nine o'clock and provide enough light for us to travel by.

The next three miles were absolutely wicked, hard on the dogs, and on Bud and me. We fought deep snowdrifts that weren't crusted hard enough to hold the sled on top. Too often the sled slid off the trail and had to be lifted back on. It became so dark that it was impossible to pick out the faint outline of the trail ahead. Brush-lined sides or the narrow road served as a guide to keep us from wandering all over the valley, and we had to let Jim pick the trail as best he could.

Finally we decided to park the sled and go on afoot. We turned the dogs loose and started off on snowshoes, calling the dogs to follow. They were reluctant, wanting to curl up by the sled and sleep. After much persuasion, however, they followed. Jim and Keno followed so closely behind Bud that they repeatedly stepped on his $10 \times 56$-inch trail shoes until his cussing convinced them that he meant it when he said, "Stay off."

Floppy and Woolie took turns stepping on my bearpaw snowshoes and tripping me. Floppy was a new dog in our team. Smoke Thomas had given him to us. I fell down five times, and it was a real effort for me to get back on my feet with the awkward bearpaws on my feet and a pack on my back. I started to cry the last time I went down. Bud cut a willow switch for me to use like a horse's tail to keep the dogs away from my snowshoes.

We arrived in a sheltered gulch where there was timber. There was plenty of dry wood and with moss and twigs from dead lower branches of the spruce Bud soon had a cheerful aromatic fire lighting our surroundings. We were somewhat protected from the wind, but still it chilled us on the side away from the fire. Our tiredness made us more susceptible to the cold. The dogs curled up in the snow, noses tucked under bushy tails.

After a time a big orange full moon rose dramatically to flood our little valley with golden light. Bud left the dogs and me with a generous supply of wood and went on to break trail to Twin Lakes cabin. He figured it would take him three hours to get there and back to us. At the cabin he scrounged for wood to build a fire to warm up, and to have

Tilling the garden.

Lenora had a green thumb.

some left for our arrival, then he returned along his newly-broken trail.

We arrived at the cabin at four a. m.. It was still warm, with glowing embers still in the stove, and enough wood to keep a fire for a few more hours. My sleep was profound on dirty ragged bedding that was there, and our one mummy sleeping bag, with our parkas to cover us. We gave each dog slices of bread, which was the best we could do for them, and they bedded down too.

Noon came before we awoke, and we were too tired to return to the sled. The sun came up bright and cheerful, and our eight hours of sleep had refreshed, but the terrible effort of the previous day left us with aching muscles and a kind of lassitude. We spent the remainder of the day seeking firewood for the cabin. The dogs took turns standing on hind legs, with paws on the window sill, peeking in to see if their food was cooking. Sadly, their pans and grub were still at the sled. Bud unsuccessfully searched the woods near the cabin looking for a grouse that he could shoot. I made a stew of odds and ends of food and a can of meat we had in our pack, and poured it over a slice of bread for each of us, and for each dog. They again curled up to sleep and wait. We all went to bed at sundown and slept for twelve hours. The dogs didn't have enough energy to do their usual howling at the moon.

We were up at sunup, and Bud and the dogs went to retrieve the sled. On his return he was laughing, saying that our tracks from sled to cabin looked as if they were made by two people on their last legs, without much hope of survival. I don't know about Bud, but I know I wasn't too sure that I was going to survive.

I cooked dog food first thing. Next we brought our groceries in from the sled, and the cigarettes. While resting the previous day Bud had found a cigarette paper partly stuck to the messy table in a drop of syrup. He carefully washed it and hung it to dry, then rolled a smoke from pipe tobacco he had in his pocket. He even shared two puffs with me.

The return trip to our cabin at Nabesna was a real pleasure for us and the dogs, for the trail was solid, and the load lighter. I could ride much of the time. I was getting toughened too, and enjoyed the physical exertion. Bud maintained a steady pace for miles.

We had left Charm at home, and she was ecstatic at our return, and we apologized to her for being gone longer than planned. She was still gnawing on frozen moose meat we had left for her.

One day after we arrived home heavy snow fell again. We knew we couldn't make it all the way to Slana, so we had to wait. It snowed, then it snowed some more. Snow didn't stop falling until there was five feet of the fluffy white stuff on the level. We needed a wind to blow the loose snow away, and for the snow to settle and develop a crust. We waited, and then we waited some more for conditions to become right for us to travel.

## IX

## BROKEN TRAIL

By the end of January we were out of Blazo for our Coleman lantern. We had also used up all of our candles, and we were out of sugar. We knew that Harry Boyden carried a few supplies for the Indians who lived on Nabesna Bar, and we had planned to buy from him if we ran short. We were too independent to go to the Nabesna Village to borrow from the Indians, because we knew they were on short supply. We didn't have permission from Boyden to break the lock on his door to get what we needed from his supply, although he later told us that is what we should have done. As newcomers, we didn't want to chance doing anything unethical. Well, I decided, I would at least make a candle from melted wax and surprise Bud.

I melted all the pieces of wax I could find from the tops of jars of jelly. I made a roll of cardboard and taped it together, put a string wick in the center, and poured the melted wax into the roll. I just knew it would make a beautiful big candle. I melted the wax, poured it into the cardboard form, then as I was carrying it across the room to set on a window sill to cool I tripped on the rug and spilled it all. The wax splattered so far and it was in such a thin layer that there was no use in trying to gather it to try again.

February days are short, and with no light to read by, the evenings seemed terribly long. In addition to what we had brought in the way of reading material there was a five-year accumulation of *National Geographic* magazines that we enjoyed. We could see to play cards by sitting close to the stove with the lid partly open, although the firelight was too poor to read by. Unfortunately it often produced smoke as well as dim light, and made the card games less pleasant.

Bud found some diesel fuel in a barrel and tried to make a light with a wick set in the diesel fuel in a pan. He rigged a vent to let the smoke out, and we ignored the fuel oil smell. Every gust of wind blew the smoke and soot into our faces. It was a good try, and we had as much fun laughing at each other's sooty faces as in playing cards. We abandoned the diesel oil light.

February 12th was a perfect day for us to start on the 40 mile trek to Slana, and we headed out in high spirits. After we had traveled two hours it started snowing again, and the wind was in our face. The dogs were eager to be on the trail, and we made pretty good speed. The trail was covered with light snow, and showed as a faint outline. Jim could stay on it, but where the wind has drifted snow across the trail the heavily-laden sled slid off. Later that day Bud had to go ahead and break trail, then return to the sled where I held the dogs. Next Bud walked beside the sled, guiding it with the gee pole. I tried it, and found it was too much for me ("Gee whiz, who invented this endurance test?"), and I was unable to keep the sled on the trail while Bud went ahead. We traveled only a few hundred yards, then I broke trail and we did fine the last three miles to the Twin Lakes cabin, with me wearing Bud's fine trail snowshoes and him wearing my round and awkward bearpaws. We arrived at the cabin long after dark. I had blisters on the bottoms of my feet, and wasn't sure I'd be able to travel on the morrow.

Next morning saw us both stiff, not very active, and I had sore feet. Bud didn't feel well, but he had to saw some wood, then break trail for a ways. We managed to travel three miles with the dogs and sled, but the snow was too deep for the dogs to travel on the unbroken trail and pull the sled. Bud lit a fire, left me with enough wood to keep it going until he returned, then he broke trail for the next six miles to the tent. Every time Bud left to go ahead to break trail the dogs howled, barked, and cried as if he had left

Lenora and Colin, June 1960.

Food was good at Tanada Lake Lodge, 1960.

them forever. Each had his own vocabulary, and voice timbre. They expressed themselves well.

Bud broke 9 miles of trail that day, traveling 18 miles to do it, and returned long after dark. I kept a huge fire going, collecting dried limbs and fallen trees. We expected the full moon to help when it came up. During the evening while waiting for Bud I tossed a huge root on the fire, and it looked like a woman's torso, with two legs and no arms. It looked spooky as it burned.

We returned to the cabin, but on the next day we made it to the tent Bud had set up, arriving late. My feet were so sore and stiff that I could hardly walk after taking off my snowshoes. Bud was tired too, but he thawed a moose steak in the frying pan and it tasted delicious to us. We finished off the meal with a can of pineapple. Bud still had the dog food to cook, but I gave up and went to bed. It takes much patience to use a dog team: food must be cooked for them every night, even on the trail, and the cooked dog food of dried salmon and cornmeal has to be cooled before it is placed in front of the hungry dogs, or they tip it over in the snow and much of it is lost.

On this trip we carried our double size Woods sleeping bag; it saved space, and was warmer than our military surplus mummy-type bags. We were overtired, and both of us tossed and turned. Frequently during the night one or the other of us would suggested, "Let's turn over, huh?"

Next morning, February 15, we awoke late with the sun high in the sky. It was very cold, and Bud leaped out of the warm sleeping bag and in bare feet built a fire in the wood stove, then he hurried back into bed to warm up. Soon the tent was warm, and the smell of boiling coffee lifted our spirits. Bud sawed down a dead tree while I cooked breakfast. His canvas and moosehide moccasins were still wet so I dried them by holding them close to the stove. Finally the canvas dried enough so that he put them on just before he headed out to break more trail. Though cold, the day was sunny and the scenery so gorgeous that I couldn't resist putting on my snowshoes and following down Bud's trail to meet him as he returned.

Bud shot a ptarmigan and had it cleaned and ready to

cook. We ate lots of these winter-white wild grouse, for they are plentiful and usually easy to get near enough to shoot. When he cleaned his .22 Colt Woodsman pistol afterward a string broke and left his cleaning rag jammed in the barrel and he couldn't push it out. He had to dig into our things and find my .22 pistol. The shotgun was too heavy to carry with all of our other gear on the sled, so we depended on the pistol for getting birds.

My snowshoes would twitter and squeak like birds as I walked along the trail, mile after mile amidst the great stillness. The dogs walked along pulling steadily, following Bud who was ahead on snowshoes. The moon came up bright, and the stars were out. We got a different view of the great white peaks on either side of us with every mile we traveled. There were so many hills to climb that we were almost too tired to enjoy the lovely white world around us.

At long last, 17 miles from Slana, we reached a permanent tent frame with a tent on it that Boyden had built. At the start of winter he put the double canvas over it, and he used it for a stopover in an emergency when he traveled this road in winter with his dog team. It had a floor, stove, a generous wood supply, and a few staples in bear-proof cans. It was nearly buried by snow, with the ridge pole swayed almost to breaking. The stovepipe was packed with snow and had to be taken apart and cleaned before Bud could build a fire. Bud burned a hole in the toe of the liners for his moccasins, and I worried that he might freeze some toes again. He cut firewood while I cooked for us and the dogs, and we spent a restful night there.

Next day was a beautiful one to snowshoe a trail in the unbroken snow. I followed Bud for a couple of miles as he went on to break trail, then returned to clean up the camp. One can see so much more when traveling afoot than when in a car. I stopped on my return to camp to gaze in the direction of Tanada Lake, which we had our sights set on as a possibility for the location of our lodge.

I busied myself for the rest of the day, for I knew Bud would go a long way before returning to the tent for the night. He would break trail and then allow it to set overnight, giving us easy travel on the morrow.

I cooked the dog food and fed the team when it cooled. They were all content to sleep and rest that day, luxuriously stretched out in the sunshine. Late in the afternoon as the sun sank from sight it turned all the peaks rose-colored, and I knew it would soon be dark. We were out of candles, and if Bud didn't return soon, he would have to eat his meal in the dark. I fried moose steak and had dried spuds ready to fry, with coffee water boiling. The tent was small, only 6 × 8, but we managed. It was shelter, and being able to warm it with the wood stove maked it almost luxurious.

By lifting the lid of the stove a bit I managed to get enough firelight to see to write in my diary. When Bud finally arrived late he ate his dinner by the light of a burning log. He was terribly tired, and said he had broken five miles of trail, all in deep snow, and then returned the five miles to the tent. He said he had almost keeled over in the snow from sheer exhaustion. The year was 1949, and we didn't know about hypothermia. Bud Conkle was an energetic man who always pushed himself to his limit, and for that reason he accomplished twice as much as other men. We slept well in our warm sleeping bag that night, with our mattress of green spruce boughs.

We decided to travel the next day, February 17, instead of Bud going over all that trail and breaking it on farther. It wasn't very cold, and the sun was dim behind thin clouds. It was a good day to travel the flat five miles of treeless country. When we reached the end of Bud's broken trail I remained with the dogs while Bud went on ahead to break more trail, with the dogs resting in their traces. I was out of cigarettes, so I filled Bud's old pipe with the last of the pipe tobacco he had. I had been anticipating a smoke for hours. I lit the match and started to light the pipe, but the bowl turned on the stem and all the tobacco spilled in the snow. So much for that.

I decided to leave the dogs and sled and travel some of Bud's trail in my bearpaw snowshoes. I sank only about three inches on the packed trail and moved easily, enjoying myself. After I had gone two miles I remembered that Jim had the bad habit of chewing on his harness, and that sometimes he tangled it, and even slipped out of harness at times. If he did any of these it would put Bud into a bad humor. I started back, but all along the trail going back I wrote messages in the snow for Bud.

I had a nice fire burning when he finally returned, and I was proud of myself for I had gathered dry branches and twigs and lit the fire with only one match. Bud was amused at my messages in the snow and said it made him feel better knowing that I was enjoying myself.

We drove the team to the end of the trail he had broken, and again I stayed with the dogs while he went ahead breaking trail. It seemed an endless task. He had to travel the distance three times: he would break trail ahead while I waited, then he would return, still packing the snow down. Then he would turn around and sometimes walk ahead of the team on the trail he had just broken.

I built a fire again, and made hot bullion tea. I drank too much of it and it made me feel ill. Bud enjoyed the bullion when he returned, with our last piece of bread. He had broken trail to within a mile of Bucko and Dorothy Thompson's cabin at Rufus Creek and had seen the lights of their cabin.

It was cold and dark when he returned for me and the dogs. I didn't feel like going on, but Bud kept encouraging me, saying it was only a short distance farther. The miles were tough, and twice I felt like giving up and settling down in the snow and staying there. Bud was on the gee pole to help the dogs pulling in the fresh snow, and the loaded sled kept sliding off the packed trail. He was tiring too, and we finally left the dogs and sled when we reached the end of the broken trail.

The dogs were content to stay with the sled as we snow-shoed off. I was wearing the bearpaw snowshoes, which were ill fitted for the deep snow. Bud broke trail for me, snowshoeing with Charm draped across his shoulders: Charm had ridden in her box on the sled that far, and now she got special treatment.

We topped a hill and looked down at the Rufus Creek cabin. The light in the windows looked so inviting and we were eager to get there. Then, suddenly, the light went out. We had about a mile to go, and it seemed to take forever.

When we neared the cabin we yelled. That brought barks and yips from the Thompson dog team, and the Thompsons, who had gone to bed, leaped up and were excited to see us. They had worried about us being trapped by the deep snow, and Bucko had planned to start up the road looking for us next morning.

Hot coffee and cookies and a warm fire with friends made it all seem worthwhile. Bud and Bucko went back to the sled and dogs and brought them in and fed them. It was two in the morning, when, exhausted, we settled into bed.

The next day, February 18, it was −10 degrees with the wind blowing a gale. Blowing snow obscured visibility and drifted in the trails. We knew that old sourdoughs would know better than to travel in such weather, but after a late breakfast of sourdough hotcakes we decided to press on the last six miles to Slana. The weekly bus to Fairbanks was to come by the following day, and I needed to be on it. Bucko had recently traveled to Slana, so the trail was good except for drifts to break through, and he went ahead with his dog team to do this. He was concerned about me traveling in the wind.

Fortunately the wind was at our backs and I was dressed so warmly that after the first mile I wished I could shed the coat I had on under my trail parka. I made three miles traveling right behind Bucko, and ahead of Bud with the dogs, doing just fine. Suddenly another dog team, traveling the other way, loomed up out of the blowing snow. It was Harry Boyden. He was happy to see us, and to see that we were all right. Like Bucko and Dorothy, he had worried about us. He was pleased to learn that Bud planned to return to our cabin at Nabesna while I went on to Fairbanks. He decided to wait and travel with Bud. Harry had hired an Indian boy to return to Nabesna with him to help break trail. They had tried twice, but the weather was too bad, with deep and blowing snow each time. Sadly on his trip from Nabesna to Slana it had turned very cold and he had had to shoot his dog Pal, for her teats had frozen (she had recently had pups) and she would have died in agony. He turned around and went back to Slana with us.

As we neared Duffy's tavern Bud saw that the tip of my

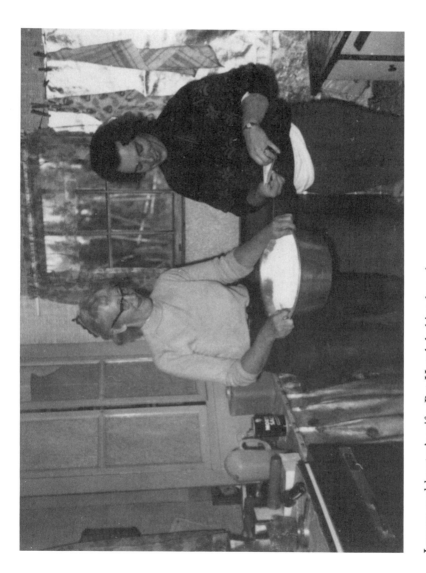

Lenora and hunter's wife, Pat Hotel, baking bread.

nose and my ear lobes were white, starting to freeze. With bare hands he thawed them, saving me a lot of pain.

Harry was staying at the cabin of his friend Knute Petersen, who was away trapping, and he invited us to stay with him. As we reached the roadhouse, however, a Trooper's car pulled in, driven by Turk Mayfield who was going to Tok. He invited me to ride with him. Bud and I dashed into Duffy's post office and grabbed our mail, and we rushed over to Petersen's cabin where Harry had a good fire going. I sorted my mail out from Bud's, kissed him goodbye, and wished him luck trapping, then I left for Tok with Mayfield.

An Army Colonel by the name of Kensley was with Mayfield, on an inspection trip. He was from Del Mar, California, and it turned out we had acquaintances in common. We hit a snowdrift at the Ahtel Creek bridge, and the two men got out to shovel our way through. Wind was blowing a blizzard across the bridge, and visibility was limited. I sure enjoyed riding in that nice warm new car and watching it eat up the miles. It beat breaking trail inch-by-inch and mushing stubborn dogs!

We stopped at the Road Commission camp at Bartell Creek and were served cake, ice cream, and coffee. The Colonel remained there to await Army transportation sent for him from Anchorage. "I don't mind waiting as long as I'm close to a stove and a coffee pot," he smiled.

Mayfield stopped at every cabin along the Tok Highway, checking on people, delivering mail, groceries, spare parts for gas lanterns and such, and relating the latest news about people up and down the road. It was an enjoyable ride in a comfortable car and I met some interesting people.

Mayfield left me at Tok Lodge run by Lee and Erma Evans, where there was electricity, a shower, sheets to sleep between, and where I didn't need to put wood in the stove to keep warm. Finally I had time to read the mail from home that I had gotten at Duffy's.

Next morning the temperature was −44 degrees F. at Tok. I telephoned my shop at Fairbanks and the lady running it for me was happy to hear from me and to know I was still among the living. She and others had sent many messages out on Tundra Topics for me, asking me to phone. But she had had no word after Harry Boyden had reached Slana and called her for me. He had told her that I'd be arriving in Fairbanks in a few days, which, of course, was my intent. I hadn't reckoned with the violent winds, the deep snow, and terrible cold that came after Harry had left, and our total dependency on dog team travel.

There's a quote I know not from where that "Only the keen and careful can hope to survive in the wilds." Bud often quoted his version: "The alert and practical will survive." We survived, and I felt we had been practical. But alert? Maybe.

At Tok the bus arrived and I climbed aboard. George, the driver, had been driving the route for ten years, and he knew everyone. He shopped in Fairbanks for most folk along the highway, and related the latest gossip as he delivered. He even knew who was sleeping with whom, and was delighted to pass the information along. My ride to Fairbanks was interesting, educational—and full of juicy gossip.

An Indian woman, leading a husky dog on a chain, boarded the bus at Tanacross and rode to Gerstle River. George made the woman put her bundle of dried fish in the baggage compartment, but the aroma of the fish still penetrated the entire bus. Charm, in her box on the seat beside me, stared at the big husky with her yellow eyes as he walked down the aisle past us with a disdainful sniff.

At Fairbanks I plunged into the routine of my drapery shop, doing work that had gotten behind, paying bills, ordering materials. While I was involved in that Bud was laid up at Knute Petersen's cabin at Slana for five days with badly swollen feet. Boyden waited for him, and the two drove their dog teams together on the two-day return trip home. The trail was firm and it was easy for the dogs to pull the supply-loaded sleds. Harry still had his "valuable brief case", the weary old flour sack filled with mail, bank statements, and money.

Bud made the return trip with four dogs: little black Spookie was gone. She had gotten loose and had fallen into a trap. Her leg was so badly injured that she had to be put away. I missed her on my return.

Alone except for the dogs, Bud completed his first trapping season at Nabesna. When beaver season closed at the end of March, the Nabesna Road was open, and he drove the Jeep to Fairbanks to sell his furs. The first thing he bought with money from the furs was a pair of light weight snowshoes for me. He took great glee in burning the bearpaw shoes so that neither of us would ever be tempted to use them again. Bearpaw snowshoes have their uses I suppose, but they sure weren't meant for the deep light snow of Alaska's Nabesna country.

Bud had also purchased the Rufus Creek Cabin, furnished, and with traps and some groceries, from Bucko and Dorothy Thompson, knowing it would be a good base for us as we started to develop our lodge, which we planned to build at Tanada Lake.

At Fairbanks Bud patiently waited for me to finish my last few orders and to sign papers turning the business over to a buyer. I enjoyed the drapery shop, as well as Fairbanks, but it was clear to me that my life now was to be in the bush with my husband.

## X

## CHARM'S NINTH LIFE

After I sold my shop in Fairbanks we returned to the Nabesna country and moved into the Rufus Creek cabin that we had bought from Bucko and Dorothy Thompson. Shortly, Bud accepted the offer of a job as heavy equipment operator for the Alaska Road Commission. Wages were good, and we needed a grubstake. Neither of us were crazy about him working. Both of us wanted to get on with locating a site and building our lodge, but that required money.

Daily, Bud drove the Jeep from Rufus Creek to Slana to go to work. One day while he and the Jeep were at Slana an ice jam lifted the wooden Slana River bridge from its footings and carried it, still upright, downstream half a mile. There it sat intact until put back in place in late fall.

However, that closed the Nabesna Road to wheeled traffic for about six months.

Knute Petersen, an old-timer who had lived at Slana for many years—he prospected summers and trapped winters—let us live in his cabin at Slana (population ten) that summer. On his first day off Bud took Keno with him, crossed the Slana River in our three-man rubber raft, and hiked to our Rufus Creek cabin. There on the front porch to greet him was our black cat Charm. The day we had hiked out in the early morning after the bridge went out she was nowhere to be found and we had had to leave her. Bud arrived back in Slana with a big pack full of our posses-

119

Charm and her kittens enjoy sunshine on the cabin roof.

Charm following her friend, the horse.

sions, and Charm draped across his shoulders atop the pack. He said that when he occasionally put her down to walk she stayed so close under his feet she would almost trip him.

That summer of 1949 whenever Bud got a day off from work we crossed the Slana River with the raft, ferrying our dogs and the cat in turn, and then hiked the five miles to our Rufus Creek cabin to spend the night. On our jaunts to Rufus Creek we often saw fresh grizzly bear tracks, but no bears bothered the cabin.

The dogs finally accepted Charm although she continued to hiss a warning to any dog that came too close. Charm hadn't been long at Knute's cabin with us, when a huge black tom cat who lived at Slana overcame her hissed warnings and spitting receptions, and before the summer was gone she proudly let us know she was to become a mother. It wasn't long before six black kittens romped across our bed at night, raced underfoot, swung on the curtains, and displayed their talents at finding whatever was put away from their sharp destructive little claws. Through it all she was a tolerant contented mother and she ruled her brood like a queen, teaching the kittens what they needed to know. She was lightning quick fury to any dog that came near one of her kittens.

When friends or chance acquaintances expressed the desire to own a kitten, they found themselves departing with their heart's desire, and our kitten supply dwindled to one little tom. In August Bob and Ruth Wilson and Joe and Lillian Heffron, friends from Fairbanks, (Bud had worked with both men at Ladd Field) drove down to spend time with us on a camping and fishing trip. We camped at a secluded spot on Station Creek on the Tok Highway, a tumbling mountain stream that gurgled and lulled us to sleep at night after we had yarned around a flickering campfire.

Our friends headed up a canyon to explore an old mine, while Bud, with sled dogs Jim and Keno, and I followed a glacier stream bed between two canyons, stepping over fallen logs and pushing through thick brush. Occasionally we crossed the stream on a fallen log, with the two dogs creeping along behind Bud with their bellies almost touching the log as they maintained balance.

High in the mountains and far across a canyon Bud spotted a silvertip grizzly and her yearling cub, and we took turns watching them with binoculars. Mama bear was busily digging a marmot out of its den, and she seemed to tear up half the hillside as she worked. Her cub sat on its haunches, ears forward, waiting for the marmot to surface. The sun warmed our backs as we watched, until the bears gave up and wandered out of sight.

On our return Bud was in the lead as we rounded a slight bend. Suddenly he motioned for me to be quiet and grab the dogs. He pointed to a hillside, not 200 yards from where we had sat watching the sow and cub. There I saw the biggest grizzly bear I ever expect to see. He was in a blueberry patch slurping up berries, leaves and all.

The bear was above us, which gave him an advantage. Bud carried his .30–06 and I carried the .30–30. Nevertheless that bear was so huge that the rifles looked awful puny to me. We decided to get out of the canyon by easing along quietly and slowly through the trees, hoping he wouldn't catch our scent. I prayed that Keno wouldn't pick this time to bark at a squirrel.

I was too scared to look at the bear through binoculars, and I could see him clearly enough without them. We eased along quietly, careful to not step on dead branches. Both dogs were so close at our heels they were almost tripping us. As we passed directly beneath the bear Bud dropped to one knee and looked at him through the scope of his rifle. I was almost paralyzed with fear, thinking he was going to shoot, and what if he just wounded it? All I could think of were the tales I had heard of how much lead a hunter could pour into a charging grizzly before it died.

Bud stopped to check the number of shells he had in his magazine, and the snick of a cartridge as he eased it into the chamber broke the stillness like a shout. Still the bear didn't look our way.

"I feel like putting my foot on the rifle and forcing more shells into the magazine!" he joked.

He told me to pick a tall tree ahead and to be ready to climb it. "I'll hand you your rifle and you start pouring lead into the bear as soon as it gets close if my shots don't stop it. If he charges us he'll come down the slope like a freight train!"

"He looks as big as a freight car with short legs," was my response.

"Don't worry about me. I'll climb a tree too if I run out of shells," Bud said. "I just wish we didn't have the dogs with us. They could stir up some real excitement."

We continued to move away from the bear, with a tall tree always in mind as a goal in case the bear discovered us and charged. Bud kept watch on the bear.

There wasn't a whisper of a breeze to waft our scent to the bear. Nevertheless it raised its nose in our direction and sniffed the air, then started walking in the same direction that we were, remaining some distance above us.

"Oh oh, he's going to meet us at the end of this canyon," Bud guessed.

That fat old bruin stayed 200 yards above us on the hillside and followed us all the way down that canyon. It was perhaps a twenty minute walk, but it seemed like hours to me. I refused to look to see what the bear was doing. Instead I asked Bud, "What's it doing now?"

"Sniffing in our direction like he isn't sure of what he's smelling. Maybe he's trying to identify us. When did you take a bath last?" he grinned.

Somehow the dogs seemed to know about the bear, for they slunk along at our heels without looking at it.

"What's he doing now?" I asked Bud, who had lingered behind to look.

"He's sitting in a blueberry patch on his fat rump pulling the whole bush up to his mouth. Come watch. He's funny," Bud replied.

"I don't want to watch him. I've seen all of that bear I want to see, and I just want to put distance between us," was my emphatic reply. I hiked on around the bend and had to wait for Bud. When he didn't come for some time I got nervous and when he did arrive I was unhappy with him.

"Where have you been?" I demanded to know, sharply.

"Looking for a log to put across the creek for you to cross on," he explained.

"Never mind the log. I jumped the creek and so did the dogs. You didn't know I could jump that far, did you?"

He laughed at me, and I admitted, "Neither did I," knowing that under ordinary circumstances I would never have been able to jump such a distance.

Bud later told friends that heading down the canyon away from that bear was the only time he remembered me keeping up with him. I think I expected the bear to follow us, so I kept looking behind, and every time Bud stopped I bumped into his packboard.

It was nine o'clock and dark when we arrived at the most welcome campfire I ever expect to see. That night I took exception to Bud's selective use of the facts, particularly when he described to our friends my suddenly discovered jumping ability.

No doubt that big grizzly bear was the one that residents along the Tok Highway and others had seen off and on for the previous two years. It hadn't been known to bother anyone or any cabins, and it mostly stayed well back in the hills.

On August 30th that year Knute Petersen had a tragic encounter with a grizzly. We were still living in his cabin at Slana, preparing to move back to our cabin on Rufus Creek as soon as the Slana River bridge was replaced.

Knute came by one morning to say hello, and to tell us he wouldn't need his cabin for some time yet. He was leaving on a prospecting trip into the hills. It was two months before we saw him again.

When Knute was mauled by the grizzly he was evacuated to Anchorage, but for several days there was no word on whether he had survived. He was a mighty tough Dane, and he survived due to the immediate response of many who helped get him from Ole Hoagland's isolated cabin on the Slana River and out to the airport at Chistochina, 40 miles over rough roads, where a Tenth Air Force Rescue airplane from Anchorage awaited with a doctor and nurse. A good medical team at Elmendorf Air Force Base Hospital had

Tanada Lake.

him on the operating table for ten hours, sewing and repairing the damage caused by the grizzly. It was 70 days before he was released from the hospital and returned to Slana.

I accompanied Bud and others who went to the area where the bear had mauled Knut. Bud picked up a piece of Knute's scalp with hair on it that was about four inches across. The whole story of the mauling was written in the blood and pieces of Knute's blue denim shirt, with bits of Knute's flesh where the bear had bitten it off. The tracks of a sow and two cubs were found. During the mauling Knut hadn't seen the cubs, so it is probable that the sow had the cubs up a tree or elsewhere when she attacked him on the trail where it went through a willow patch.

We cared for Knute's four dogs until he returned. He had raised them from pups, and they worked and behaved well for him. They worked well for us if it suited them, and they watched for opportunities to get into fights with our dogs. I had to carry a heavy stick to help Bud break up dog fights. When our dogs and Knute's were harnessed into one team there was no limit to the load we could pile into the sled, and often both of us could ride. But if Bud wasn't out front to grab and tie dogs up while I stood on the brake or anchored the sled with the tie rope, the fight would be on, with all the dogs in a snarling, snapping, melee. We would almost have to knock a dog out before it would give up and lie down. Experts told us to always hit a Malemute on its head because that was the only part he didn't use: if a club hit his back, feet, or legs, it could slow him down in his work.

It was important to get the fights stopped before a dog was crippled, and usually the first thing a fighting sled dog grabs is the leg of his opponent. Once Bud was standing amidst all the dogs as they were viciously trying to tear each other apart when he tried to whack the big dog that had started the fight. At the moment that dog had Jim by the throat. Bud let loose with a hefty whack just as Jim shook himself loose, and Jim caught the glancing blow.

Bud later said he was sure that Jim thought the blow came from the other dog. It didn't make it easier on Bud, for Jim bit his hand. Bud leaped back, trying to get away from the snapping teeth that seemed to surround him, but he tripped and was suddenly beneath all the fighting dogs. In the end he had to actually knock three dogs unconscious to stop the fight, and he felt lucky to get out from under that swirling mass of fighting dogs with only that deep bite from Jim.

Charm was too wise to trust Knute's dogs, although they paid little attention to her other than to cock their ears forward to watch when she was in sight. Our dogs had all accepted her, and now she could even ride on the sled without being in her box. She sat alongside the sled while it was being loaded, then jumped aboard and curled up in the hollow space left in the tarp covering purposely for her.

Bud returned to the cabin one day to find Keno curled up on our bed with the cat. He looked resentful when he was told that sled dogs didn't belong on beds, but outdoors in a cold dog house. It was easy to read his expression as he left: "How come that cat gets to sleep there and I don't?"

In late November, while Bud was busy on his trap line, I rode the bus to Fairbanks to sell the log house we had bought there. The Army captain who had rented it was being transferred, and we had found a buyer.

When I was ready to return, Bud drove to town with a few furs to sell and to drive me back with him. He loaded his furs and dogs into the Jeep, but forgot Charm. She must have been off hunting. He was deeply apologetic when he explained to me why she had been left. Mice were abundant near the cabin, so she would easily manage until our return, he assured his unhappy wife.

We arrived at the Rufus Creek cabin after Bud had been gone about a week. Charm wasn't there. Harry Boyden stopped by to chat. He had been at our cabin two days after Bud left, and Charm had come down from her quilt-lined box high on a shelf of the porch. She hissed a warning at his pup, drank the milk he set out for her, followed him for a bit, then she was gone. He remained overnight, but didn't see her again.

I walked far out into the woods in all directions calling her name, but to no avail. A few days later Bud discovered unmistakable cat tracks on the road, many miles from the cabin. The animal had been headed away from the Rufus Creek cabin, toward our old home at Nabesna, 34 miles away. I became convinced that she had gone there to see if we had moved back there without her.

There was no easy way for us to get to our old Nabesna cabin: the bridge was still out, with our Jeep on the Slana side. There was too much bare gravel on the road to use the dog sled. Also, at the time we had to drive to Valdez to get an order of winter groceries, due in on a ship from Seattle. We had to be on hand when it was unloaded. This was a three day trip, with shopping, visiting, and the long drive both ways.

When finally we arrived back at Rufus Creek there sat Charm on the porch looking unconcerned and independent. If ever I wished an animal could talk it was then as I stroked her luxurious black coat while she nestled in my arms purring. What experiences and loneliness she must have endured on that long determined journey. How many close calls had she survived? What did she think upon reaching the cabin at Nabesna to find no trace of us? Do animals feel the same intensity of loneliness and disappointment that humans do?

When we again saw Harry Boyden he told us there had been unmistakable signs that Charm had been at the Nabesna cabin. There were cat tracks all around the cabin, he said. No one else in the area owned a cat that we knew of.

In mid-December my cousin Harvey Steele drove out from Anchorage with his shiny new Buick station wagon. We were to ride with him Outside (to the South 48 states) for a Christmas visit. We loaded the dogs and dried salmon food, while I explained the facts of life to Charm as I put her in her box in the Jeep. She was going to spend the time with the Thomases, as were the dogs, while we were gone. They had even told me that Charm could sleep on their bed. Smoke and Ruth Thomas had moved back to their cabin near Jack Lake on the Nabesna Road for trapping season.

Bud drove the Jeep up the Nabesna road to leave the animals off, and assured Keno that he would return soon.

Lenora picking fireweed in bloom.

As Bud drove away he heard Keno's mournful wailing, even over the sound of the Jeep engine.

Five inches of fresh snow lay on the highway as we headed out, and Harvey sped around a horseshoe curve without slowing, and the long heavy Buick left the road and teetered on the shoulder of the narrow road. We held our collective breath and slid out very carefully on the side away from the drop off, with the car precariously balanced. We stopped a truck to pull it back onto the road, and two hours later we were again on our way—at a somewhat reduced speed.

We made it to Yakima, Washington, in time for Christmas dinner with my aunt and uncle, Charlie and Ella Steele, Harvey's parents, who owned apple orchards there. We visited elsewhere up and down the Pacific coast as well as Bud's folks in New Mexico, enjoying ourselves and the mild weather, but silly us, we missed Alaska, we missed the cold, we missed the mountains, we missed our snug little cabin, we missed our dogs and our cat.

In the four years since we had traveled the Alcan Highway there had been many changes. It was still far from the modern paved highway of today, four decades later. On our return we had to wait five days at Crows Nest Pass in British Columbia while road crews cleared the highway (not the Alcan) of deep snowdrifts. Finally we reached the Alcan, and late one evening we stopped at a recently-built roadhouse. It was late January, and the temperature had plunged to $-40$ F., and we were checked in before we discovered that the only heat in the roadhouse was the big fireplace in the center of the lobby. Each room had a half-door, which theoretically allowed heat from the fireplace to enter. We were each given two extra blankets that were as well worn and dirty as those on the double and single beds in the rooms. We shivered through the night.

My aunt and uncle had given us a box of Jonathan apples, and we had put them in the car to keep them from freezing. We had kept that box of apples from freezing for days. But that night they froze in the lobby of the roadhouse, next to the fireplace.

Harvey dropped us off at Nabesna Road and we hiked the

few miles home over deep snowdrifts. We had been home for one day when Smoke Thomas arrived with our dogs in his team. Keno was so happy to see Bud that it was hard for both Bud and Smoke to unharness all the dogs, especially Keno. Keno had reluctantly worked for Smoke, but the others had been unconcerned about who they worked for, and they had done well. Keno had sulked and whimpered and coaxed to be let loose, but Smoke was afraid that he would leave if turned loose.

Charm had refused to live with the Thomases. She remained a few days, then she had left, traveling the 20 or more miles to our home at Rufus Creek, expecting to find us there I'm sure. She arrived as the coldest spell of winter set in, with temperatures down to $-50$ degrees F., much too cold for her to get out to hunt mice or other food.

We found her, frozen stiff, curled in her quilt-lined box over the kitchen door where she had gone to sleep trustfully awaiting our return.

## XI

## PROGRESS

The $12 \times 4$ log cabin we moved into at Tanada Lake in November 1950 seemed palatial at first. That, of course, was in comparison with the tent. Before long I was wishing for a much larger area, or, better yet, another room. Bud's trapping went well that winter, and since he had no other place to skin his catch he brought them into the cabin to work by the warmth of the fire and the light of the Coleman lantern. I wasn't overly happy to see those pretty frozen little foxes and other creatures brought in to thaw, and then lose their lovely skins. I did learn to knit wool socks that winter, and I could sit with my back to Bud while he worked, or sometimes I lost myself in reading a book.

Every fur he collected meant money for us, so I taught myself to be a dutiful wife, and I congratulated my husband with each catch. I have always been willing to work, but I never offered to skin any of his catch. I never offered to learn how, although I know I could have done so easily. I'll admit there were a few times when Bud was tired and still had a lot of skinning to do that I was almost tempted to volunteer.

My cousin Harvey Steele, who moved to Alaska a few years before we did, had recently moved into the house he had built at Anchorage, and he invited us to spend a month with him. A few days before Christmas Bud picked up his traps, put the furs he had caught in a gunny sack, and we drove the dogs to our Rufus Creek cabin where our Jeep

It was a cozy cabin.

The jeep was good, reliable transportation.

was parked. We piled the dogs, gunny sacks full of furs, and enough city clothes to last for a month, drove or shoveled our way through the drifts on the Nabesna Road, and twelve hours later we were in Anchorage. The highway was gravel all the way.

The luxury of a hot soaking bath in a real tub, plus the freedom from bulky winter clothes we had to wear to keep warm in the cold-blooded Jeep, was compensation enough for the long rough ride. Anchorage was an interesting new town and we enjoyed our month there, but by late January we were ready and eager to return to Tanada Lake.

We were home by February first, and Bud was back to long days of hauling firewood and cutting it for the stove when he wasn't checking his traps. I had a generous supply of hand-knitted wool socks for both of us that I had knitted while he skinned his catch. In February and March the winds funneled down through the mountains from the south, making the fetching of wood and water challenges of courage and fortitude, and polishing the ice on the lake to a high gloss.

We had brought home with us a supply of staples, and didn't have to leave Tanada Lake until early April. Then we picked a time when the trail was good for dogs and sled to retrieve things stored at our Ruffus Creek cabin.

Prevailing winds in winter swept down from the mountains, piling huge snowdrifts near the shores of the lake, sweeping the lake ice clean of snow, and making it so slick that it was difficult to stand or to walk on.

The wind that winter was sometimes so strong it was frightening. In the severe cold it was doubly scary. On one of Bud's trips across the lake with the dog team the wind blew the dogs sideways on the glare ice, and Bud crawled to Jim and held onto his harness to help pull the team along.

This brings to mind something that lead dog Jim did to Bud. Bud and the team were across the lake from our cabin, and Bud told Jim and the other dogs to lie down and wait while he walked into the timber to check some traps. Jim knew better than to leave the place Bud had left him, but the wind was just starting to gust. Perhaps Jim thought it a good idea to get home ahead of a bad windstorm. He didn't tell me his reason for coming home without Bud when he came trotting up with a pleased-with-himself look on his face and led the other dogs and sled to where Bud always unharnessed them. I debated about taking them back to find Bud in case he was hurt or something. They were reluctant to head out again, but I had managed to get them started out when I saw Bud emerge from the far shore. I unharnessed the dogs and explained to Jim that he was in for trouble. Big trouble.

"Jim thinks for sure that I'll whip him, but I have a surprise for that dog," Bud said emphatically as he headed for the dog houses. He harnessed Jim alone and hooked him to the sled, then he got in the sled to ride and Jim had to pull him alone across the lake to where he had left his ice chisel, some extra traps, and a big lynx he had caught. Jim pulled with all his strength and if he slowed too much Bud snapped the whip at his rear to keep him moving. Where the ice was slick and hard to get purchase, Jim settled low, almost on his belly, and scratched to keep moving. He was a tired dog when they returned, *but he never left Bud again.*

Jim disobeyed orders another time and in so doing could have plunged himself, Bud, the other dogs, and a loaded sled into the icy waters of Tanada Creek. We were on our way home to Tanada Lake from our Rufus Creek cabin with a heavily loaded sled. The trail across from Nabesna Road to Tanada Creek was fair if we traveled it early morning. However it was high noon by the time we reached Tanada Creek, where in many places the ice was thinning. There was even open water where ice had fallen in here and there, in which places we traveled along the bank. We came to a big bay with a four foot high bank. The ice in the middle was thin, with open water in a wide crack.

Bud had me stand on the sled's brake to hold the team while he scouted the ice close to shore to be sure it would hold the heavily-loaded sled. If we could cross there it would save back-tracking to where we could get on the riverbank.

"Lie down, Jim," Bud ordered.

He obeyed, and the other dogs followed suit. However, as soon as Bud was directly across the bay, with open water and thin ice between us, Jim jumped to his feet to follow Bud, and I couldn't get the brake claw to dig into the slick ice. I stood on the brake yelling my lungs out, but it didn't slow the dogs one bit. While this was going on Bud ran back around the edge of the ice, yelling all kinds of directions to me and to the dogs. But the team was taking a short cut directly across to open water.

Fortunately Bud intercepted them close to the open water. As he did I turned loose of the sled and headed for safe ice near shore. Bud grabbed Jim by the collar and pulled him to the edge of the crack and poked his head in the water, explaining to the dog while he was poking his face in the icy water that if he wanted to swim, it would be best to wait until he was out of harness—that it wasn't a good idea to drag the other dogs and the sled along. Surprise: the ice held them.

I don't know how other dog team drivers break their dog teams of chasing game, particularly rabbits. Bud used a method one day that I thought was unique. While checking traps one trip he rounded a bend and just ahead of the team a big white snowshoe hare was jumping up and down with one of its big hind feet caught in a trap. The dogs headed for that rabbit, ignoring Bud's shouted commands.

He anchored the sled to a tree and hung each dog by its harness onto the limbs, with just their hind feet barely touching the ground. He killed the rabbit, removed it from the trap, and skinned and gutted it right in front of them, explaining that it was to *our* dinner, and we'd put the bones and scraps in their dog pot to cook. I regretted not being there with my camera. How ridiculous can one be with dogs? The other dogs accepted what happened, but I am sure that Jim's dignity was insulted, and likely he nursed a grudge.

One night when it was so beautiful it was almost a sacrilege to go to bed, we watched the brilliant full moon flood the world with light. Tiny diamonds sparkled from the snow, and we could see almost as well as if it were high noon. We were entranced with the silence and the beauty and watched until the bright moon drifted slowly behind dark hills before settling in to sleep. We were soon awakened by the steady yap-yap-yapping of one of our dogs.

Bud, irritated, got up to see what the yapping was all about, planning to hush the dog. The dog, and I forget which one it was, was on his house staring intently across the open tundra. It was just light enough that Bud saw a dark wolf sitting on its haunches 150 yards away. He eased back into the cabin to get his rifle, but the door squeaked, alerting the wolf. He got a quick shot at the fleeing animal, but missed. He said he was too sure of the $50 check that he saw waving in front of his eyes—bounty money then paid by the Territory. All the other dogs were hiding so far back in their houses that one couldn't be sure that dogs were there. It was spring, wolf breeding season, and perhaps it was a female wolf trying to lure one of the dogs out. Any dog dumb enough to go would likely have found a wolf pack waiting to tear it to pieces.

There was much evidence of a wolf pack traveling and hunting near and about Tanada Lake. We often heard their hunting calls, but seldom found a wolf kill. We traveled only a limited part of the pack's range, so our observations didn't mean much. There were nights when we were serenaded by wolves howling in concert, and we learned to recognize the high-pitched wail of the pups. We admired the wolf, and felt privileged to share the wilderness with him. Bud certainly didn't decimate the wolf population, try as he might to trap them. He was lucky if he got more than one a season, when their pelts were prime.

Our dogs were a lot of work. Daily cooking, catching whitefish for them with a gill net, buying dried salmon by the bale, and what seemed like tons of cornmeal, all added up to a lot of work and not a small expense. However they were good company, and very much a part of our family. Too they were often a source of amusement and entertainment.

Some dogs could be very exasperating. Jim could slip his choke collar, and when he did he usually got into some sort of trouble, like the time we returned home from working all day across the lake to find he had eaten the whole pot of dog feed that we had cooked that morning and set out to

Sled dogs getting a lift.

cool. Honestly, it looked almost as if his belly dragged the ground. He had a very guilty look on his face.

Keno didn't often get into trouble, and so was never tied. One morning he was asleep on the sunny hillside and didn't see us get in our boat to cross the lake. Normally he always accompanied us. We thought it would be a kind of a prank on him to sneak away and let him be surprised when he discovered we were gone, so Bud pushed the boat away from shore and paddled a long way before starting the outboard motor.

We were half way across the lake when we looked back to see him running back and forth on the shore, howling. I watched with binoculars to be sure he didn't start to swim across, but he didn't and went back to where the other dogs were tied. We worked all day cutting and peeling logs, and Keno, looking pleased with himself, was on the beach to greet us as we beached the boat on return. Bud reached out to pet him but quickly withdrew his hand to smell it. Horrified, he yelled, "Keno, get lost you stinking thing!"

Keno had dug under the make-do canvas we had arranged around trees for a toilet, and he had rolled in the foul mess. Then he had gone to our tent home and had curled up on both cots. He had never before taken the liberty of entering our tent unless we were inside and invited him in.

We had opened a one-pound can of Darigold butter that morning for breakfast and replaced the lid. A can of evaporated milk with two holes punched in the top was atop the butter can. When we arrived back at camp to that smelly dog, and our fouled beds, we found the butter can gone, *and the can of milk was still upright on the can underneath.* I never did figure out how Keno got that can of butter out from under the milk can without spilling the milk.

It was a few days before I happened across the butter can where he had carried it, worked the lid off, then licked most of the butter out and buried the can.

That was Keno's way of getting back at us for sneaking away from him. We didn't do that again.

I'll never forget April 22, 1950. It wasn't my birthday, but then Bud Conkle wasn't a husband to remember birthdays anyway. The day was special because on it my thoughtful husband delivered, via dog sled, a lovely Monarch white enamel coal-wood kitchen range. It was a two day project for Bud to dissassemble and haul this heavy stove over the long rough trail from the Nabesna Road. He worked as hard as the hard-pulling dogs. To keep the awkwardly loaded sled on the trail on sidehills he had to run alongside and brace the load up to keep it from tipping over. Bud was a tough man, and when he decided to do something he seldom allowed complications to stop him.

When reassembled in my rustic kitchen the stove, to my eyes at least, was absolutely stunning. In Anchorage Bud had found the stove on sale, and Gezzie Freight Lines agreed to deliver it to Slana whenever they had another delivery out our way. It arrived soon enough for Bud to haul it to Tanada lake while the trails and lake ice were still frozen. Could it have been that Bud was tired of meals fried or boiled on the two-burner Coleman stove?

I am fond of wood tones, and I loved the log walls on the inside of our cabin, so I hand-scraped, planed, sanded, then varnished them. The three overhead beams were a big undertaking, but in the end I felt were worth the effort, for they came clean and finished in a lovely golden color. For a man who had never previously built a log cabin, Bud did skillful work, and the logs all fit nicely. It was my job to chink between the logs with sphagnum moss, the only material readily available. A year after I chinked them I fitted quarter-round material to cover the moss between the round logs, and years later the moss was still tight.

We made some nice improvements during our second year at Tanada Lake. Bud acquired a whipsaw from a friend who was wise enough to get rid of it. Bud built a platform to hold the logs on while we sawed. I had never heard of whipsawing lumber, but since Bud seemed sure he knew how, it was ok with me, especially if we could cut smooth boards to make a floor and roof for our cabin.

The two of us spent many long hard hours sawing. Bud worked on top, and I worked in the pit. With every stroke of the saw I was showered with sawdust. Any loose bark or pieces on the logs fell on me, and within a few minutes my hair, face, and clothing would be clogged. The man on top pulled the saw up, and the dunce underneath pulled the saw down. Anyone who ever had the creative pleasure of whipsawing lumber would have understood why, if Bud and I had parted company that summer. He accused me of riding on the handle while he was trying to pull the saw up. He even suggested I take off my boots to make myself lighter. I cried, and I don't cry easily, either. I told Bud I was trying to push the saw back up, and it was all I could manage to pull it all the way down as we sawed.

It sometimes took us an entire day to produce two or three six-inch boards that were a mere six feet long. "It doesn't take intelligence to create this kind of back-breaking labor," I would grit out at my industrious mate, and then I would walk away and sit on a stump out of his sight, wondering if a floor and a roof were really that important. He tried working the whipsaw by himself, but soon came looking for me, and, of course, he talked me into returning and we would finish the log we had on the rack.

Next day I would return to the pit, and we would end up fighting again.

Then one day by chance or luck, Bud put a log on the rack that had no twist in it, with few knots. It was a newly-dead tree, mostly dry. Sawing that log went so well that we had it cut into boards in far less time, and the sawing was much easier than the green logs we had previously worked on. After that Bud decided it best that he cut dead trees for whipsawing.

He hadn't known all about whipsawing after all, I decided. I had taken it for granted that he knew what he was about. We worked five days once, averaging four boards for each day. Once in six days of sawing we produced eight boards that were 1 × 6 inches wide by 16 feet long. When we had enough boards to cover the roof, but lacked a few for the floor, we abandoned our whipsaw. By that time we were adept at walking on the boards that weren't nailed down, and I was content to get by on them for a while longer: it was better than suffering the torture of the whipsaw pit.

On one supply run to Chitina with the Jeep and trailer we returned with groceries, three barrels of gasoline, dried salmon and cornmeal for the dogs, and some 90 pound

Quick catch for the pan at Tanada Lake.

roofing paper. The roofing paper was a load all by itself, and since it was too late in the year for hauling it in the dog sled, Bud packed it one roll at a time across the seven miles from the Nabesna Road to Tanada Creek and the boat. I packed 40 pounds, Bud 80, and in addition he carried a five-gallon can of gasoline in each hand. Still he forged far ahead. He would put his load down and return and carry mine. We would then sit for a time, both our arms waving like automatic windshield wipers, swiping at the mosquitoes that were so enthused over dinner arriving at their doorstep.

I remained at the cabin while Bud spent three days relaying supplies from the Jeep. He took his small tent and camped overnight wherever he was ready to sleep. On the first night he camped near a pothole lake and was awakened at dawn by loud splashing and slurping noises, and peeked out the tent flaps to see a young bull moose in the lake, submerging its head under water to feed on aquatic plants. It paid not the slightest attention when Bud folded the tent and left. On arriving at the boat Bud was taken aback to see that a grizzly bear had eaten the ends off a roll of tarpaper. However the bear had left enough so that, with another roll, he could patch and cover the roof.

The trash pit we dug didn't fill very fast. We had little to dispose of, for we used everything we could, and some items had several uses. For example the few Darigold butter cans we had tossed into the pit were rescued, the bottoms cut out and the sides cut open. The long slender pieces of tin were perfect for nailing down the edges of the roof to prevent the fierce winds from ripping the tarpaper loose. While the tin was bright and shiny it was a bit decorative besides being useful. Even after rusting through it lasted until we could afford better roofing.

## XII

## WILDERNESS BABY

For two years we were as busy as the beavers who were our only neighbors at Tanada Lake. We cut and hauled logs across the wide lake, built a cabin, cleared brush, trapped in winter, and made occasional trips out for supplies. We were both happy with our lives.

So satisfied were we in the big-little-world we had created for ourselves that it came as a huge surprise to learn that before another winter passed there would be another Conkle to share our Tanada Lake haven. Had I been much younger the surprise would not have been so great. Our hopes and prayers were for a healthy child with the same love of adventure which we so enjoyed in the rolling caribou hills and sky-scraping mountains that surrounded our lovely lake.

We had discussed the possibilities of acquiring an airplane for transporting hunters and fishermen to Tanada Lake from the Nabesna Road once we were established and ready for business. Bud wasn't a pilot, therefore he needed to take time off sooner or later for flying lessons. The practical thing was for both of us to return to Fairbanks—for me to have our baby, and for Bud to learn how to fly.

In June 1951 we sadly boarded up our cabin, pulled our boat onto the bank a short distance down Tanada Creek, turned it over with the motor under it, and covered it with brush. With our Trapper Nelson packboards and each of us leading a dog and three running loose, we hiked the seven miles to the Nabesna Road where our Jeep and trailer were parked. We boarded up our Rufus Creek cabin, and headed for the city for an indefinite stay.

Our five sled dogs went with us. Two were obliged to ride atop the loaded trailer. They were an amusing attraction all the way to town as they precariously balanced themselves sitting on their haunches, red tongues lolling, as they took in the passing scenery. Fortunately for my pride we stopped to unload at long-time friends Henry (Hank) and Edith Ernst's place on the outskirts of Fairbanks. It would not have bothered Bud in the least to have driven right through the center of town with that ludicrous load except for the fact that he so intensely disliked city traffic.

We lived in a variety of houses. First we built a $9 \times 14$ wannigan—a small cabin on skids. Running water meant running to our neighbor's house to get it. We were accustomed to going outside to the outhouse, except the one at Tanada Lake was larger and well stocked with magazines, and with a beautiful lake to look upon and we never closed the door. Soon we moved into a friend's house. He was away, but trying to sell it. It was a comfortable modern house but with improvised fixtures that we had to learn how to use. This took a lot of experimenting, and then repairing of the damages we had caused before we learned and could go on to the next fixture. The house lay under the traffic pattern for airplanes flying from Fairbanks International Airport. We soon became used to the sound of light aircraft skimming over, but the shattering thunder of the big ones taking off on midnight departures always brought us bolt upright in bed.

There were other city ways to which we had to adjust, such as the steady stream of drunks who sang, yelled, or cursed as they strolled by. The telephone rang all hours and callers usually asked for people we didn't know. Our sled dogs were accustomed to the wilderness and cared not for our neighbor's peace; they seemed to choose after midnight to do their howling, requiring one of us to leave bed to hush them. Noisy traffic and sirens added to the bedlam. We were soon homesick for the peace of Tanada Lake.

Every morning Bud spent an hour taking flying lessons at

Boating the dog sled.

Weeks Field from his instructor, Hawley Evans. Hawley had to remind him frequently, "Conkle, you're not flying a bulldozer. Don't be so rough; handle those controls more gently."

That fall Bud went with Cleo McMahan, a well-known guide, as an assistant guide conducting trophy hunters from Outside on a big game hunt. He needed the experience plus the recommendation of a registered guide in order to take the examination for registered guide himself.

Bud and Johnny Cross, the friend in whose house we briefly lived, together bought a vintage Stinson L-5, an airplane used by the military for reconnaissance during World War II. Bud had his student's license, and he and Johnny flew out on a moose hunt. Johnny knew a good place to land, and they were to be gone two days. When they didn't return on schedule I called Cliff Alderfer, a Wien Airlines pilot, who flew out to see what had delayed them. They had broken a propeller, and one from an old airplane that had once belonged to famed pioneer pilot Harold Gillam, plus a few minor repairs, took care of the problem and they flew the plane home loaded with moose meat.

Johnny's Cross's house sold, and we moved back into the wannigan. Bud contemplated building an addition to help us get by until spring. The baby was due October 2, but there had been no action on that front by mid-October. Our good friend and my doctor, Dr. John Weston, learning of our living arrangements, offered us use of a furnished bungalow four blocks from downtown. No charge. We gladly accepted with relieved and thankful hearts, and boarded our dogs at a kennel.

Bud got a job working nights for the Northern Commercial Company at their power plant shoveling coal into the furnaces, and shoveling ashes out and hauling them away. It was a dirty, tedious job for a man who loved the out-of-doors. The pay was fair, and we needed the money.

On October 22 we had a six-pound red-headed baby who we named Colin.

We again moved, this time to a house with no close neighbors, where we could keep our dogs. We had been there a week when the furnace quit in the middle of the night. The outside temperature was $-30$ F. In the morning the third repairman I called agreed to come, but it was Sunday and we had to pay overtime rate. The furnace ran for a week, and then quit again, also in the middle of the night. Another Sunday morning call to a furnace repairman brought me such a gruff refusal that I would have preferred to face a grizzly bear rather than talk to that man again. Next call brought a pleasant repairman who came and fixed the furnace with no fuss. That furnace later paid off during the coldest part of January when a power failure lasted long enough to produce pipe-freezing temperatures in many homes. That furnace was designed to run without electricity, and it did, although at the time of the power outage I was concerned lest the sparks from Bud's explosive language set the house afire.

Fairbanks' houses in those years were full of quirks, cranky furnaces included. Among other things we put up with were: having to carry hot water out to pour into a sink and washing machine drain to thaw it every time before using it; a leak in the bathroom washbowl hot water pipe—we turned it on only when in use; a bathtub drain that had rusted through; a vent with a fan over our sink on which I pulled the chain to open the vent to yell at Keno who was howling. We'd yell "Shut up," loudly, and he couldn't figure where we were yelling from. It worked, at least for a while.

Early one Sunday Keno started moaning and wailing so that we couldn't sleep. I jumped out of bed, climbed onto the sink, yanked the chain to open the vent, and it came off in my hand, leaving the lid open with icy air rushing in. I closed it temporarily by wedging it with a coat hanger. Standing on the sink in a thin nightdress did little to improve my disposition.

We had a Frigidair refrigerator that froze everything. One day I washed my hair at the kitchen sink. With suds all over my head and eyes shut tight my elbow broke through an old crack in the porcelain sink, allowing soapy water to soak everything on the shelves below. The kitchen light switch had a short that no one seemed able to fix; it had to be flipped two or more times before it remained on. I half expected the short to catch the wall afire.

Freighting fuel and Aviation gas from Valdez over the Thompson Pass.

We were offered better living quarters, utilities furnished, in exchange for my taking care of a new business. It was a pickup point for a clothes cleaners. I could do the mending and repair jobs involved. We happily moved in and boarded the dogs again, except for Keno, our pet. But Keno wanted to be in the house, which isn't good for a sled dog. He howled and wailed when tied outside. Friends from Slana visited briefly, and agreed to take him back with them to keep until we moved home to Tanada Lake.

A new electric range sat in the kitchen of our new quarters, but it needed a special plug before it could be hooked up. When the plug arrived days after we moved in it was the wrong one. I cooked on our old two-burner Coleman camp stove. Days later two men came to connect the stove. After a couple of hours of fussing about they turned the power on and a wire blew and smoke poured out of the stove. They said they didn't know how to fix wires inside the stove, but would send another man over.

We had invited out-of-town friends for a turkey dinner. They arrived while we were waiting for the stove to be fixed. I had to cook potluck on our camp stove instead of a turkey dinner.

On a Sunday, Bud's day off, he found the switch box at the rear of the shop, shut off the power, and had me stand by to turn it on again when he was ready to try it. He tinkered with the stove, and within minutes had the burned-out wire repaired, altered wires to the plug, plugged it in, and had me turn on the power. Surprise! Everything on the stove worked.

I was still standing in front of the stove planning my first meal when suddenly all the lights went out. "Ye gods, what now?" was my reaction.

Then came a loud knocking at the door. The irate landlord demanded to know what Bud had done to blow all the power—he had seen us at the switch box, and now all his power was off. Bud was speechless.

The phone in the office rang and I went to answer it just as a customer walked in and she commented that all the lights on our block were off. "Wow, we're in for trouble now," I thought. Mustering up my courage, I called the electric company to inquire.

What dramatic timing for a power failure that included our section of town!

We preferred the hard work that it required to survive at Tanada Lake to the frustrations and inconveniences of living in town. However, life was good. Bud completed his flight training before the deep winter cold set in, and received his private pilot's license. Our baby son was healthy, growing, and active. The secondhand Weasel, a military surplus tracked all-terrain vehicle Bud had purchased soon after our arrival at Fairbanks, was completely overhauled and ready for use, a job Bud accomplished in his spare time.

City friends frequently ask what motivated me to move so far from civilization, especially with a baby. Simple. It was a life style we had come to love. It is true it was challenging, but not as challenging sometimes as we found city living to be.

Come spring it was time for us to move back to the bush. We arrived at our Rufus Creek cabin, and reorganized before our journey home to Tanada Lake with our weasel. With this new machine we expected the seven mile trip to be almost a pleasure, compared with hauling ourselves and our supplies by dog team.

## XIII

## RETURN TO TANADA LAKE

April 28 1952 was a beautiful spring day for traveling from our Rufus Creek cabin back to Tanada Lake. The Weasel rolled effortlessly over the tops of the hummocky tundra that I had sweated over and sworn at so often when Bud and I had backpacked over the same route. Baby had a snug bed in a cardboard box, and he contentedly slept most of the way. Bud had made one trip in with a load of supplies so we knew the cabin was all right.

We ate a picnic lunch on a sunny hillside while watching the dogs run free, two at a time. We saw no game that they might be tempted to chase. Freedom. We felt it. We had room to stretch. We had privacy. No one was jostling our shoulders, we heard no airplanes overhead, no loud cars roaring, no sirens. There was no telephone. The serene mountains, still deep with winter's snows, poked high into the clear blue sky as they always had. Our minds and souls began to relax from the tenseness acquired from ten months of city living.

At home—and we now regarded our cabin at Tanada Lake as home—we set up the crib at the foot of our bed, found a niche for the high chair and a place for the chest of baby clothes, and the little one was part of the household at Tanada Lake. Our activities were scarcely hampered by his presence. All four sled dogs and Mr. Jones, the cat which I had acquired in Fairbanks, were as happy as we were to be at lovely Tanada Lake.

Bud went right back to work cutting, peeling, and hauling logs across the lake. On nice days I took the baby, Mr. Jones, and Keno and went along to help. When weather was good I put Colin in a playpen beside the cabin while we peeled logs, or cleared the place for the new addition to our log cabin.

By May 10, after two weeks of working with logs it was time to go to Slana for the mail. Light snow was falling, but we loaded the Weasel anyway, bolted the heavy door, and headed down the lake. Snow fell more heavily, and the wind picked up. By the time we neared the lower end of the lake in the slow-moving Weasel, snow had drifted, obscuring the lake ice. Bud watched the best he could, hoping there were no weak spots. It was late in the season, and time for the ice to start melting. I sat tense, thinking we would all drown for sure if we went through the ice. Heck, that couldn't happen; we hadn't even made out a will. We made it to the tundra crossing without mishap, even though the wind blew so hard it was unpleasant traveling.

The Weasel engine died on the Nabesna Road, six miles short of the cabin at Rufus Creek. We were out of gas. Bud had put in what he was sure would be plenty. We had no choice but to hike the rest of the way. I wrapped baby in a blanket and put him in the packboard on Bud's back. I put diapers and a bottle in Bud's pocket and the rest of what we needed in mine, thinking, "Here we go again, hiking the Nabesna Road. Just like old times." We hadn't brought our snowshoes, and we could have used them in the deep snow—which was deeper than it was at Tanada Lake. Neither of us was in good hiking condition after our winter in town.

As usual Keno was at Bud's heels and he was good entertainment for the baby, keeping his attention until his little head drooped and he fell asleep. He was warm and protected from the wind. After four miles of steady traveling in the deep snow we were near the end of our endurance. Bud built a fire in an old gravel pit and we warmed the baby's bottle and were pleased to see what a little sourdough he was: he seemed to be enjoying the situation, and had kicked up no fuss.

The snow stopped falling, the wind let up, and the bright sun came out, lifting our spirits to no end as we started off again. Baby was laughing at Keno trailing along behind until he fell asleep. However when we got to the last mile he became tired of all the traveling and protested loudly. Bud yelled back that he was going to go on. I was walking more and more slowly, and stumbling in the frozen moose tracks and breaking through the crust into two feet of soft snow.

When I reached the cabin Bud had a fire going, he had changed his son and fed him, and had tied him into a chair by the fire. It had taken us six hours to walk the six or more miles from the Weasel to the cabin, and I was dog tired.

When we got to Slana Bud found a check in the mail for furs he had sold. We drove on to Meiers Lake, near Paxson on the Richardson Highway to visit Cleo and Daphne McMahan and family. Bud had told Cleo he was interested in the J-3 Piper Cub that Cleo had and was thinking of selling. One of the mementos in my scrapbooks is a cancelled check dated May 12, 1952, made out to C. B. McMahan in the amount of $1,200, partial payment for J-3 Piper Cub with a Lycoming 85 horsepower engine, wheels and floats included. On June 12, one month later, we paid the $300 balance due and we owned J-3 Piper Cub N42126.

On the return home from our May trip to McMahans Keno jumped from the Weasel and one track ran half over him. He yelped, and Bud reversed and backed off. He wasn't badly hurt, but limped for a few days. He rode inside the rest of the way home. It was a long trip back, for the ice on the lake was unsafe for the Weasel, and we had to go the long way around the hummocky tundra. The baby was a good little fellow all the way, and when he was ready for his bottle we warmed it near the exhaust pipe. We left the Weasel on the gravel bar on the lakeshore and walked across the ice to the cabin.

As we neared the cabin we saw fresh tracks of two caribou cows that had been headed toward the upper end of the lake and the mountains. After we had been home four days I looked out a window and there saw a caribou cow standing on the lake with a tiny wobbly calf nursing. Moments later the second caribou appeared with her newborn calf at her heels, trotting toward the lower end of the lake. The mother had her head up and she was sniffing. It was touching to see her little calf running with the same long stride and easy gait of its mother. I'm sure she smelled the smoke from our cabin, as did the nursing cow, for that one also bolted, half-dragging the still sucking calf a few feet until it turned loose and ran with its mother.

Bud and I watched the wild game around our lake with never-ending delight. We knew the caribou cows left the herd in order to give birth each year, and we wondered if they went into one of the many long timbered canyons that run out of the mountains. Would those two cows, and in a few years their calves, return to the same place next May? Two days later Bud found their tracks where they had gone into the timber, and not too far distant, he also found tracks of a big wolf. Those two caribou mothers with their tiny calves looked so alone and defenseless surrounded by the vast wilderness where lurked meat-hungry grizzly bears and wolves.

What an amusing assortment we traveled with. For a time it was one black cat and the sled dogs. Now travel was much easier in the Weasel with four dogs, one gray cat, and one baby. Mr. Jones, our new cat, traveled like a veteran. When we were in Fairbanks he seemed to select us to be his family. He got along well with Keno, and was well mannered. He had a way of almost apologizing if he did something he wasn't supposed to. His name came naturally; when he wanted in he would pat the door and it almost sounded like someone knocking. I would open it and say, "Well, come in Mr. Jones."

We were happy to have a cat again because mice had moved into the cabin in our absence. I explained to Mr. Jones that it was his duty to do something about them, and he did. He caught mice at night but played with them so long and noisily that for a time we didn't get much sleep. We watched him put one in Bud's slipper once, then pull it out again and turn it loose to chase it all over the cabin. When it gave up the ghost he caught another, and played with it until it was no longer interesting because it was dead. I didn't toss Mr. Jones out with his dead mice because I had seen evidence of mice in the baby's bed.

Despite the almost daily rains that came after we arrived home we kept faithfully at digging to level the ground for our new addition. The ground was frozen—permafrost it is called—and when the insulating moss and ground cover was removed it thawed only a few inches a day. Bud spent long hours peeling logs and he was busy setting up a sawmill across the lake, and clearing moss and leveling a spot for a tent site. He had two resident bear hunters booked for a fall hunt, and it was important to have a place to bunk them. With the sawmill he figured he could saw enough lumber to build a floor and put siding up for a base for the tent.

On May 28 it snowed four inches of wet heavy snow, but it immediately started to melt. Bud went across the lake to peel logs and I took time out from washing baby clothes and digging dirt when the baby was asleep to watch two cock ptarmigan fight on the sunny slope beyond our high cache. The ptarmigan were so tame that they came right up to the cabin. Keno completely ignored them but the cat would sit twitching his tail, watching. The hens must have been sitting on their eggs, for I seldom saw them around. The cock in charge of the area closest to the cabin sat in a tree by the hour, calling and talking in that odd rolling noise ptarmigan make. Far away on another hillside a second cock answered from time to time.

On May 30 the sun came out reluctantly about noon and I put the playpen on the sunny side of the house to corral Colin, for he maneuvered very fast on all fours, and knew no limits. I did the laundry outside, on a scrub board. No automatic washer and dryer at this resort. The freedom of living our lives the way we had planned them, and working how and when we wanted to, made up for the lack of conveniences.

Bud left early that morning to drive the Weasel to the lower end of the lake where he planned to leave it. When he was ready for another mail and supply run to Slana he walked to the Weasel on the lake ice. Once the Weasel was

Colin and his best friend.

parked he went on down Tanada Creek to get the Aluma Craft boat to bring it upstream, for the ice was gone out of the creek. He caught four grayling for our supper, and took pictures of two bull caribou that carried impressive antlers already—big bulky things in full velvet. As he drove the Weasel down the new trail he had brushed out over a period of two days, he discovered the remains of a huge bull moose. The story was clear—there were grizzly tracks, and a great mound of dirt, moss and leaves atop what was left of the moose. Fresh wolf tracks skirted the mound. The moose was probably killed by a grizzly before it went into hibernation.

On June 2 I climbed the mossy well-worn path to the top of our look-out knoll and glassed the surrounding country, searching for game, and incidentally to watch Bud and the Weasel slowly creeping across muskeg swamps and timbered slopes on the far side of the lake. Bud had gone to Slana the previous day, but I had so many things I wanted to accomplish that I stayed home.

He parked the weasel on the lakeshore and walked across the ice and was at the door with his heavily-loaded packboard much sooner than I expected. Mail day! It took precedence over everything else. After I had read my mail Bud told me who he had seen and what they had said, and gave me the latest news from Slana. On his return with the Weasel a young bull caribou with small antlers had run alongside, wanting to challenge the moving vehicle. He shook his antlers and pawed the moss, then trotted ahead to repeat the threat. Finally he gave up and bounced off into a timbered hillside.

On a warm sunny day in early June we put the playpen and blankets on the toboggan and Colin in Bud's pack and I crossed the lake to help with the sawmill assembly, and in peeling logs. Keno and Mr. Jones followed. Ice next to shore was rotting, so we took the two-man raft along. I peeled logs while Colin rattled the sides of his playpen, trying to shake it loose, making clear that he didn't like being confined. Bud set up the Rube Goldberg sawmill not far from the whipsaw rack where we spent so many long hours the previous year sawing lumber for the roof and floor of the cabin. I hoped the sawmill produced more boards with less effort.

We ate lunch in the sunshine by a crackling fire. Colin went to sleep and I fished where a creek runs into the lake and had melted the ice back far enough so I could drop my line into deep water. My fishing produced two fresh grayling for our supper. Wind came up, dark clouds rolled across the sun, and it started to rain. Colin went back into Bud's packboard, wrapped in a blanket. I pulled the toboggan, with Mr. Jones and Keno following. Two blue eyes were all that showed from inside the dark blanket covering Colin as the rain soaked the rest of us, but the babe laughed and enjoyed the ride.

One day an Army plane circled the lower end of the lake, then flew around the upper end. They spotted Bud out on the ice with the yellow life raft, circled over him and flew low over the cabin, and made a smooth wheel landing on the ice near Bud. It was a U.S. Army reconnaissance Cessna 180 with two men and a pilot who were surprised to find us so far from highways and any village. They refused an invitation to visit our cabin for coffee, but promised to see us in a few days. They planned to return with a Weasel and five men to camp at the lower end of the lake for a few days.

A few days later Bud left early in the morning to walk down to open water to check on the boat, and to catch lake trout for our supper. The five Army men were just coming along the trail as he arrived, and they had a visit.

On June 12 we had our first company of the season. I saw Keno with his ears up looking intently across the lake. Two of the Army men were there, yelling for Bud to come and get them. The ice had melted so far from the shore that he had to take the life raft to ferry them from shore to the ice, and again from the ice to our shore again. I had a fresh dried-apple pie which went over big with the coffee we served. I was shy about opening my mouth because I had a front tooth missing. The previous day a front tooth had come loose from my dental bridge, and none of the glues we had would hold it in place, then I had lost it. These young Army men were enjoying the fishing and the scenery for a few days, and said that when they left they would leave what canned goods and groceries they had left under our boat at the end of the lake.

Log peeling was growing monotonous, so a day or so later Bud went to the lower end of the lake to fish for lake trout and to see what the Army guys might have left under our boat. He feared a bear would get to it before he did.

One morning Keno awoke us early with loud barking and we fell over each other getting out of bed and to the door to see what had disturbed him. Keno stood looking across the open tundra, his hackles up. There we saw a dark grizzly, and it seemed to be considering whether to approach closer to the cabin. Bud yelled and the bear ran for cover.

That day we continually glassed the open countryside, but we didn't see the bear again. Late that day we saw caribou grazing on a far hillside, white shoulders and rumps glistening in the late afternoon sun. On most evenings, when wildlife was active, we took binoculars and sat on Lookout Hill and glassed for game, enjoying our remote wilderness picture show. Usually we saw moose and caribou, occasionally a grizzly bear, sometimes a wolf or a fox. Usually we saw beaver swimming near their dam at the upper end of Tanada Lake where a small stream emptied into the lake. The beaver had built their dam up this creek a short distance, but commonly swam into the lake to get willow and other branches and trees to tow home for their winter food supply.

By late June Bud had the creosote-treated foundation logs in place for our new $14 \times 18$ addition. The logs were notched for floor joists. Between us we had peeled enough logs to lay a full round. It excited us to see such progress. It was a project to move and to lift into place the logs for the long wall, for they were 20 feet long, and 8 to 10 inches in diameter at the butt. Bud had towed most of the logs we needed across the ice with the weasel. When the ice melted too far from shore he had to wait until the ice was gone so he could tow them across with the boat

On June 27 came the Tundra Topics message from Cleo McMahan that, "Bud Conkle at Tanada Lake can now pick up his J-3 Cub." We had hoped the ice would be gone far enough so we could tie the plane in front of the cabin where

Home sweet home at Tanada Lodge.

we could watch it from the window. The ice hadn't gone yet, so we had to anchor it in the open-water cove at the far end of the lake for a few days.

Bud couldn't wait, but left at 5 a.m. the morning after we heard the message, drove the Weasel the six miles to the lower end of the lake where he parked it, walked the seven miles to Nabesna Road and drove the Jeep to Meiers Lake on the Richardson Highway. He stayed the night with the McMahans to help put the floats on the Cub and then he flew it a bit before flying home. He left the Jeep there, to be retrieved later. The flight home took him two hours.

I had been working out-of-doors and went inside to see what kind of mischief Colin was up to, when I heard an airplane in the distance. I rushed out in time to see the low-flying yellow Cub circle the cabin. I could see Bud's big grin as he waved. He then flew to open water at the lower end of the lake to land. I rushed to get binoculars and ran to the top of the hill and, while mosquitoes feasted on all my exposed flesh, watched Bud's first float plane landing at Tanada Lake. He was to make hundreds and hundreds of such landings on floats and with skis over the coming years, but that first landing was a thrill for both of us.

## XIV

## A ROAD TO TANADA LAKE?

A track on the Weasel needed repairing and it was time for a mail and supply trip to Slana. We decided it was a good time for all three of us to go. Rotting ice had drifted and was touching shore on both sides at the narrowest part of the lake, with no easy way around it. Bud pulled and I pushed the heavily-loaded Aluma Craft across the ice to open water. Aluminum in the boat bent in two places, and I was sure it would break and leak, but it didn't. Eventually we arrived at the cove where the Cub rode at anchor. It looked so pretty, its bright yellow outline reflecting on the quiet water of the sheltered cove.

Bud wanted to take us for an airplane ride, so after he carefully inspected and went through all his preflight requirements, I climbed into the rear seat and he handed me the baby. We wondered what Colin's reaction would be to the airplane, but he paid no more attention than if he was on my lap at home. Little did we know that as an adult Colin would become a skilled professional pilot.

The little plane broke free of the water, rose, and circled the lower lake, then headed across the trail we had so laboriously traveled so many times. I was amazed to see Jack Lake under our wings within twelve minutes. On foot backpacking, or with the dog team, it required the better part of a day to travel that distance! I decided right then I was going to like flying.

I had frequently wondered what the tops of the flat hills

Stocking the pantry.

bordering the lake to the northeast looked like. On our return to Tanada Lake Bud flew over them, and I looked down on caribou there where they were grazing on a mossy meadow. He gently eased the Cub onto the lake and it was soon re-anchored in its sheltered cove, while we faced the ordeal of having to travel in the rough-riding old Weasel the same route over which we had just whizzed in the plane. And I had thought that the Weasel was luxurious after using a dog team!

We transferred everything from the boat to the Weasel, with me sitting under mosquito netting to keep Colin out of reach of the bloodthirsty insects. On this trip across the tundra in the Weasel on July 1, I was fascinated by the beautiful flower display from Mother Nature that lasts such a short time each year—short days of glory and color. There were dainty elfin bells of shaded pinks of the most delicate hues on slender stems; tiny pink bell-shaped blooms on the thick and scattered blueberry bushes; purple blooms on tall stems; pretty little yellow northern buttercups; many scattered wild dogwood, with white petals and yellow centers that resembled strawberry blooms; clusters of wild bluebells; solid bunches of tiny vial-shaped blooms of I-know-not-what-flower; there were purple to deep lavender clusters on tall stalks, including one area perhaps a half mile square of solid purple blooms that somewhat resembled the thistles I knew in California.

Sadly, a few days later on our return most of the blooms were gone, with a few straggly petals clinging to their stems. However, the wild roses were just budding and ready to bloom. The Weasel traveled at a crawl and I leaned far out watching, writing my notes, wishing I could pick each type, find a book to identify it, and examine it closely, but time was important and we had to keep moving.

Bud repaired the Weasel track at the Rufus Creek cabin, where he had tools and parts. One evening while working, with the evening air vibrant with clouds of mosquitoes swirling about his head, a car stopped, and the people chatted with Bud, asking about the Nabesna Road. While talking, Bud ignored the insects that hummed about him, while the two women and two men used a spray bomb every time a mosquito came near. Their arms constantly waved as they slapped at the vicious bugs.

"Do you have mosquito repellent on?" one of the ladies asked Bud.

"No, ma'am, But if they get much worse I'll put some on," he replied. This brought a gale of laughter from the travelers, and even Bud had to smile. The mosquitoes couldn't have gotten much worse.

Bud was convinced that it would be easy to tow the Jeep across the tundra hummocks into Tanada Lake behind the Weasel. He wanted to use the power take-off of the Jeep to run the sawmill. He planned to have me steer the Jeep while he drove the Weasel. I planned to find a man to do that job. However, on the morning of July 3 we started out from the Nabesna Road across the tundra with the Jeep behind the weasel with me steering it, just as Bud had planned. It was much easier than I thought it would be, and all was going smoothly until two miles from Tanada Lake, in the middle of a swamp, one of the tracks of the Weasel (not the one Bud had just repaired) broke.

Repairs were too big a job to tackle with the tools we had with us. The mosquitoes descended on us in clouds, and Colin, asleep until this point, took a notion to howl his impatience. I plopped him into his daddy's packboard with the mosquito net covering him. I put what I could carry in my pack, and we started across that old familiar trail. I hadn't forgotten some of the uncomplimentary words I had used so many times before when a tall hummock or wiggly clump threw me off balance and down I went into the cold swamp water. The wet legs of my blue jeans clung, making it doubly difficult to be agile. Bud stood on the far side on dry ground yelling advice. Even with the baby jumping up and down in his pack he could kind of run across the tundra and keep his balance, but I never could.

I was filled with disgust, for we were supposedly now modern, with a fine rebuilt Weasel, and a new (to us) airplane. Yet here we were, again fighting our way step-by-step across that miserable, rough, wet, hummocky, mosquito-infested tundra.

We walked over a rise along a good game trail. Keno's ears came up and he bolted, paying no attention to Bud's shouts. He disappeared into the nearby timber, and almost immediately returned, traveling even faster, his tail between his legs, speeding in our direction. Right behind him came an angry cow moose followed by her tiny calf. The cow didn't seem to be much perturbed by our presence, although she left off chasing Keno, crossed the trail ahead of us with her calf by her side, and with long easy strides soon spanned the rough tundra and a steep uphill climb to reach the timber. How I wished I could travel Alaska's rough lands with such seeming ease.

Keno was too wise to come within reach of either of us during the balance of our hike to the boat. The business of loading the boat and getting it out in the water away from the bugs was all that saved Keno from being forcibly reminded—again—that he wasn't to chase moose. Especially a cow moose with a calf. Perhaps he got the message from that cow; her ears were back, her hackles were on end, and she looked positively evil as she had rousted Keno out of the woods. Perhaps he knew she could and would have killed him with those sharp front hooves if she had caught him.

We delayed briefly where Tanada Creek drains the lake and caught two lake trout for our supper. We always left our fishing poles in the boat so had them on hand when they were needed. We found the airplane just as we had left it. Bud was tempted to fly it home and let me run the boat the rest of the way, but then we saw a bull moose swimming across the lake. He sped the boat up and closed with the moose, attempting to get pictures. Then the moose turned and swam toward us, shaking his paddle-like antlers. We retreated. The bull climbed ashore and stood watching us. Rotten ice extended the full width of the lake, but it was too rotten to walk on, so Bud had to push a channel through.

Mr. Jones, the cat, was at the dock to greet us and he was so happy to see us that we could hardly walk without stepping on him. He had eaten all the moose meat and cooked food I had left him. That night the fresh lake trout

It was a family business.

fried to a golden brown and accompanied by the first greens from the garden made a satisfying meal for the Conkles who were happy to be back home.

To those who live in southern climes it might seem incredible that winter ice commonly remains in Tanada Lake into early July, but it is so. It was July 5 that year of 1952 when the ice was finally gone sufficiently for Bud to fly the J-3 Cub and land it on the lake in front of our home. By then we had two more rounds of logs up on the new addition, and the doorway was cut out and framed. It was a big project to notch logs with the chain saw to fit the new logs to the old cabin. I couldn't bear to watch, for sometimes the screaming saw hit a knot and flew up into the air. I can see where the man handling the saw (Bud) could easily get hurt. Bud assured me he could handle it, and I returned to my work.

Our mail brought a letter from my cousin Harvey Steele telling us that he and his wife Hazel planned to fly to Tanada Lake in their 85-horsepower Aeronca Champion to spend a few days with us on their honeymoon, and they wanted to do some fishing. We were sound asleep at one a. m. one morning in early July when an airplane flew low over our cabin. We jumped out of bed and ran out in our nightclothes in time to see the plane fly out of sight around a point and circle in preparation for landing in the big bay. The water was glassy, which made depth perception difficult for a pilot, and we knew Harvey could judge where the surface was more easily by watching the tree-lined bank.

I went to get dressed and while doing so Bud yelled that he had heard them hit the water, and it sounded as if they were in trouble. He could hear the engine still running at high rpm's and the plane wasn't getting any closer. He put on pants, urging, "Let's get going. We've got to take the boat and see what is happening."

The Aluma Craft was at the lower end of the lake, and we had a clumsy wooden boat at the cabin, with one paddle. Light was dusky, and the world looked unreal and hazy as we paddled as fast as we could toward the sounds of the engine. As we neared we saw the plane with one wing tip almost touching the water. The plane was turning in ever-

After freeze up the jeep could be driven over the lake ice.

widening circles, moving farther from shore with each circle.

Finally, when it neared the shore where we were frantically paddling, the prop hit one of the floats, making the most awful racket, and Harvey turned the engine off. Bud let me out on the bank and paddled toward the crippled airplane. Hazel stood on a float and yelled to Bud, "Hurry, we're sinking!"

Bud reached the plane and tied a line to it and towed it ashore. Harvey had misjudged the water surface and had hit hard on one float, which had bent one wing-lift strut. The plane was in no danger of sinking. The prop had cut a neat slice through the top of one float, bending the propeller tip, but there was no damage to the plane that couldn't be easily repaired. In fact, Harvey flew it home after Bud and Harvey completed the repairs.

Bud and Harvey flew in the Cub to the lower end of the lake, planning to have Harvey bring the Aluma Craft and motor back to the lodge. They were gone all day and by ten that night Hazel and I worried that they had met with an accident. When they returned we learned they had hiked to the Weasel and repaired the track, and had towed the Jeep the rest of the way to the trail by the lake. Bud was back with the airplane half an hour before Harvey returned with the boat.

Our first fishing customers arrived over the weekend while Harvey was still with us to help Bud with the flying. With a tripod they lifted the wing of Harvey's Champ and repaired the lift strut. They patched the float and straightened the bent propeller tip. Both planes flew to Jack Lake on the Nabesna Road to bring in two young Army couples from Eielson Air Force Base. One couple had a two-month-old baby and a four-year-old boy. Two small babies here, far out in the wilderness? Yes, and they presented no problems. In the years to come there would be others.

Comfortable tents were set up for our guests, and everything went well. Fishing was good, and the weather was beautiful. Then suddenly, everyone was gone, and I was alone at Tanada. Bud had flown to Slana for the mail after his last trip of flying our guests out to Jack Lake, where they had parked their car.

I hardly ever thought about our isolation, and I was never lonesome. While Bud was gone on this trip, for the first time I could remember I wasn't interested in working at any of my unfinished projects. Nothing I read held my interest. I finally took Colin with me to a lovely grassy slope where I sat in the sunshine and with binoculars studied the distant hills and ridges, searching for game.

The game animals around the lodge appeared to show off as soon as our company left, a peculiarity we noticed many times over the years. I watched a loon on the lake as it tried to turn a large grayling so he could swallow it headfirst. The loon held the wriggling fish by the middle, and without letting it loose, it somehow maneuvered it a bit further toward the head with each wiggle. Finally it had the still-flipping grayling positioned in its bill headfirst, with most of the wildly flapping tail still out. That loon looked to me as if it had bitten off more than it could chew. It gurgled and choked and flopped as if it was having difficulty in breathing, then it shook its head as if it was trying to rid itself of something too large to swallow.

While the loon was finally getting the oversize fish into its belly a young bull moose strolled down the path from the outhouse, walked under the high cache, and stopped to look us over until Keno spotted it. He went barking past me and chased the moose a short distance, then came back with his tail between his legs and went into his doghouse. I think he was only being protective. Why didn't that moose show itself for our company? They had asked if ever we saw game near.

Bud got another round of logs up on our addition, then decided we would go to the lower end of the lake to complete bringing the Weasel and Jeep to our sawmill site across the lake. Both vehicles were loaded with supplies. We got an early start and I was steering the Jeep while Bud towed with the Weasel. Colin stood in front of me, his little hands on the wheel, steering wildly both directions, and objecting when I overpowered him and got us back on track. We had traveled but a couple of miles when a twin-engine Grumman Widgeon circled low over the lake, waggled its wings at us, and landed.

We met the plane on the beach and discovered those aboard were from the U.S. Army at Eielson Air Force Base. Unaware that anyone lived on the lake they said they had flown out to look around, and to do a little fishing. Two of the boys offered to help Bud drive the Jeep, and another said he would take the baby and me back to our cabin with our boat. Bud thanked them and said I was doing ok, and didn't mind. He said that. I didn't. The pilot said they would drop by in a couple of days as they left.

They did stop in, and during the conversation the Captain dropped a bombshell. "You'll probably be happy to know that the U.S. Army is planning to build a road from Nabesna Road to the outlet of Tanada lake, near Tanada Creek," he said. "A survey crew will be coming soon. When the road is completed the Army plans to build a recreation camp at Tanada Lake for Army personnel."

You could have heard a pin drop. Bud's face was a picture of horror.

"You can't be serious," Bud finally said, his face pale.

"You mean you don't want a road in here?" the Captain said, looking puzzled.

"Lord no," Bud said, explosively. "We've chosen a good fishing lake where there are no roads. This is to be a fly-in lodge—or hike-in for those who want to. But a road would destroy us."

The Captain was crestfallen and puzzled. I'm sure he thought we were a weird couple. In that year of 1952 roads into isolated lakes and wilderness country were considered progress.

That survey crew never did come to Tanada Lake. We carefully watched the Army's plan for a recreational camp at Tanada, and much to our relief President Eisenhower took the stand that the Army already had enough recreation camps in Alaska. No funds were ever appropriated for a road—a road that would have destroyed our dream of establishing a wilderness lodge at Tanada Lake.

## XV

## MORE GUESTS

The sawmill worked! It ran from the power take-off on the Jeep, and by July 22 we had enough lumber for the floor and three-foot-high sidewalls for our two 8 × 10 tent frames. Bud hauled the lumber across the lake with the boat a little at a time. One sunny day we took a picnic lunch and crossed to the sawmill, but I wasn't much help unless Colin was asleep. The baby was so active that it kept me busy keeping him out of where he didn't belong. He was already walking.

I managed to catch a 14-inch grayling and a three-pound lake trout to take home for our supper. We never tired of these fresh-caught fish, for they tasted so good and made a good meal.

Back at the cabin Bud rushed in for binoculars and showed me a large very dark brown grizzly bear sauntering along the open hillside a mile or so above the timbered bar where we had the sawmill.

"I wonder where he was while we were at the mill? Did we run him out of the timber, or was he just passing by? I sure hope he shows up when I get some hunters in September," said Bud.

We watched until the bear went out of sight.

Bud worked long hours building the floor and sides for one tent, and then he put the white canvas over the frame. He built a door for it, and with two cots and a stove inside, it was almost like a small cabin. We were delighted to have it

177

Packing supplies.

A dog, small boy and perfect club house.

ready for the two sports fishermen we expected over the weekend. But come the weekend morning when Bud was to take the Cub to Jack Lake to pick them up, a thick fog lay on the lake.

"Why is the weather lousy when we get customers?" Bud demanded to know, impatient and discouraged. We badly needed the paying customers in order to buy more supplies.

By noon the fog lifted enough so he flew to Jack Lake, although the tops of the mountains were obscured. The route he flew was at low altitude, and Bud knew every inch of it. Patches of blue were showing by the time he returned with the first fisherman. The two had been late leaving Fairbanks and they hadn't been waiting long. I was so proud of the smooth landings as the little yellow Cub settled on the glassy water and taxied to the bank to discharge the passengers and a beaming Bud.

I fed the men, Bud had the boat ready for them, and they trolled for lake trout and fished various areas of the lake for the rest of the afternoon and late into the night. They were a happy pair when they came in to clean their catch. The colors on the lakes and the mountains were as beautiful as I had ever seen them. Lavender and green velvet mountains reflected in the clear blue water, and the evening skylight cast soft shadows in ever-changing colors across the vast panorama. The beauty wasn't lost on our guests, for their praise was prodigious for Tanada Lake, the magnificent setting, and the good fishing.

Bud finished the frame and floor for a second tent. It sat near the first, its screened door facing the lovely view of the lake. Two more rounds of logs had been added to our new room, and it was time to go to Slana for mail and supplies. Colin and I went along in the Cub—a new experience for me, to fly for mail and supplies. Maybe I wouldn't have to backpack home afoot this time.

It is a 30 minute flight from Tanada Lake to Cobb Lake, the closest lake to Slana where Bud could land. It was a mile uphill through scraggly spruces and underbrush from Cobb Lake to the Slana-Tok Highway. The only place we could beach the Cub and tie it safely was a tiny bay a quarter of a mile farther.

We securely tied the plane to near-shore trees, after yanking the floats as far up on the bank as we could, with the nose pointed out. We hiked the mile and a quarter to the highway through hordes of mosquitoes, then hitch-hiked a ride to the post office and trading post at Slana.

We visited with friends at the roadhouse after reading our mail and buying supplies. Fred and Inez Bronniche, who lived nearby, invited us for lunch, and after a nice lunch and visit, Fred drove us back to where we could hike back to the plane. He offered to help us carry what we had, but we declined his offer. I carried the packboard holding Colin, with his diaper bag and bottles slung over my shoulder. Bud's pack weighed close to 100 pounds.

Wind had picked up by the time we left the highway, and there were whitecaps on the lake when we reached the airplane. The plane was rocking and bouncing and straining at the ropes with each wave. Water was washing completely over the floats. There was no chance of getting airborne in such wind, and we had to stay with the plane and do what we could to keep it in the water and headed into the wind. The wind could easily have flipped it if it hadn't been securely tied. I sat in the front seat to add weight to the airplane, while Bud stood on the floats, getting soaked from each wave. It took a lot of maneuvering to get us aboard with the plane rocking the way it was.

After a couple of hours we started to time intervals between the heavy gusts of wind. Each interval lasted two or three minutes longer. When we timed those intervals at five minutes, Bud said if I could help by getting out and holding the plane back against the shore so he could untie the ropes and prop the engine into life (we had no electric starter on the Cub), we could get airborne and get out of there. Otherwise we might have to spend the night there.

"Ok. And when the engine starts please don't leave me standing on the bank," I agreed rather nervously.

Colin had fallen asleep or I would never have been able to leave the plane—he'd have been pulling at the throttle and everything within reach, with possibly disastrous results.

I laid him on the seat and fastened the seat belt over him, then got out on the bank without falling off the float into deep water. We had rehearsed what each of us was to do, for once the plane was untied it would be at the mercy of the wind. When Bud untied the ropes, we were both to hold the plane until that gust abated, he would rush to prop the engine into life, and I was to climb aboard as he spun the prop. I planned to be in my seat with the baby, fastening my seat belt, while he was in the front seat after the engine started, and he would taxi into the wind.

It worked. I was frightened to death. The door on the Cub opened in such a way that if the baby had awakened and started to crawl out he could have fallen into deep water. As I stood outside the plane I watched the open door, expecting to see that little red head appear at any moment. He was so active and quick that I just knew something terrible would happen.

It was a wonderful relief to be airborne again, and although the air was turbulent most of the way home, our lake was as smooth as glass when Bud gently touched the floats down near our cabin.

Mail on that trip brought Colin a bunny rabbit that when inflated was big enough to ride. It had long ears and a painted face with big whiskers. Colin hated that fake rabbit with a passion, and he cried every time I blew it up for him. Growing up he never feared grizzly bears or anything else, but he never did make friends with that rabbit and I finally put it away. When he was much older he found it, pumped it up with a tire pump, and shot it with his dad's .22 rifle.

One morning I heard Bud swearing so fluently that I rushed out to see what catastrophe had overtaken us. He was just picking himself up off the ground, angry because his heel-less leather boots had slipped on the wet ground of the steep trail. Bud seldom fell or stumbled, and when he saw me coming he exploded, "If I wasn't so equipment poor I could buy boots that fit instead of these blankety blank oversize clumsy things that make me trip over my own feet."

He had lost a heel from his leather shoes on the day he had left to go to McMahans to pick up the airplane, and he

Super Cub recovered from Lake, 1963.

Retrieving the weasel.

hadn't gotten around to locating a new heel to nail on. Not long afterward the heel came off his other shoe, so he was walking around with no heels on his shoes. The trail to the lake down the bank in front of the cabin was steep, and it was slick when wet. When his feet went out from under him, as it did frequently when he was nearly out of decent footwear, I heard a few new words added to his already expressive vocabulary. He threatened to take time out to make heels, but he didn't do it. While this was going on I realized I should take time to put new patches on Bud's shirt and jeans, which were only precariously clinging to his body. I chose this time to quote a saying I found in an old Dutch cookbook I own: "He who hunts and fishes must wear ragged clothes." That brought a wry grin from Bud.

Each time I thought we had a little money ahead and could order at least two pairs of pants and a shirt for Bud we had to have money for equipment repairs. This time it was for the sawmill. The belt lacing had broken and Bud had laced it with moosehide strips to get by until the mail arrived with repair materials.

Bud had been at the sawmill one day when a high wind suddenly came up. The waves it churned up on the lake swamped the boat. The nine horsepower Evinrude motor had bounced off the transom, but the safety chain held it to the boat, or we would have lost it in deep water. Bud had to wait for the wind to die before he could paddle home. When he got home he was much relieved to find the airplane riding at anchor as he had left it.

He had to overhaul the outboard motor, for it was full of sand. Luckily it didn't need any new parts, and once back together it ran as good as new. While he worked on a tarpaulin on the beach near the airplane overhauling the outboard, a mama duck and her brood of eight swam unconcernedly around the floats of the plane, paying no heed to him. She quacked loudly when Keno arrived on the shore, ears up, looking at her.

The mallard had brought her newly-hatched little ones to our place as tiny balls of fuzz. She lived under the boat dock, and I think she believed it was a safe place for her ducklings. She paid no attention to us, but if a hawk or an eagle flew over she quacked and headed for cover under the dock. One day she suddenly swam away from shore, clearly alarmed. I investigated and found Mr. Jones pacing the beach, looking flustered and outsmarted. He knew he was in trouble if he even looked at the ducks, so he ran for safety under the cabin and sulked the rest of the day. I didn't see him again until next morning.

The last weekend of July was busy. I cleaned the cabin and cooked meals while Bud flew in four fishermen who spent two days with us. I had bread and pies to bake, and in the midst of my busy time Colin developed a severe two days of diarrhea. However, fishermen are easy to cook for because they spend most of their time out fishing. We had a fish fry, and I served new lettuce and carrots from our garden. Too there were fresh rolls right from the oven, with lots of red current jelly. We picked them in a draw only half a mile from the cabin, and Bud always accompanied me with a rifle when I went to pick, for bears like the currents too. I loved the berry-picking outings, which includes blueberries, and Bud always helped. The jams and jellies and pies that resulted were delicious. Most visitors commented on how well we lived, not realizing how much work it was for us to achieve that status.

I didn't mind the long busy days when we had clients or friends for two or three days at a time, but I was mentally and physically exhausted after they left. I think it was because I had adjusted to being alone for long periods of time. I didn't have what I considered any leisure time. Every moment was filled with something to do, or something I should be doing. Reading became so much a part of my daily routine that I felt my day wasn't complete without it, but it was difficult to find time to read when people were at the lodge, and it was a minor frustration to me.

There were times when I got up very early in the morning on beautiful days and went to the top of Lookout Hill to enjoy the scenery for the peace and contentment it seemed to radiate. In the early morning the dark shadows of the timbered slopes blended right to the water's edge, affecting a compelling, quiet, beauty. The lake sparkled with a thousand jewels as the shimmering sunlight spread an ever-widening path from shore to shore, while here and there a fish broke the surface, leaving tiny ripples. Each of those ripples danced and sparkled, catching the reflected sunlight. A lone duck, tiny on the vast lake, might dive for its breakfast and come up in a different spot to leave its trace of dancing ripples for a few minutes.

August 2 was Bud's 40th birthday, and though his main present was two weeks late, he still considered it very special. It was his registered guide license which arrived rather prosaically in the mail. Bud had to take the examination twice, for his score the first time around was low. Paper work was not one of his great talents; hunting and woodsmanship were. After all, our plans and work so much depended on his getting that license, that we almost expected a special U.S. Fish and Wildlife Service airplane to deliver it. The success of our lodge depended upon Bud being able to offer guided hunts from the lodge. With the airplane and the guide license, all we needed were clients for the hunting season. Summer fishermen had started to arrive in fair numbers, but the income per fisherman wasn't as much as it was for a guided hunter.

In early August Bud had another busy weekend flying fishermen to Copper Lake. They set up their own tent and cooked for themselves. The wind was so gusty and strong most of that day that I ran to the lookout to watch with my heart in my mouth whenever I heard the Cub. It frightened me to see how the wind bounced it around in the air; once I saw it drop suddenly, and lift again. But at Jack Lake where Bud picked the men up he said it was calm. He admitted he was glad he didn't have a passenger when he hit the downer I had seen.

He remained at Copper Lake until late at night waiting for the wind to die some before flying home. I spent a long anxious day wondering if he was waiting out the wind, or if he had had an accident.

On August 12 Bud was waiting for weather to improve to fly to Fairbanks for a hundred-hour inspection for the airplane. The wind was blowing a gale as it seemed always to do when he needed to fly. He got up three times during the night to check the plane where it was bouncing up and down on the waves that rolled ashore.

While waiting for the weather he put more logs up on our new addition. The floor joists were notched and set in place, and we had loose boards spread across the joists to walk on until Bud could get the roof on. For the floor we planned to haul ⅝-inch plywood in with the Weasel. I could hardly wait to expand into the new room, and in my mind's eye already had it furnished.

After a two day wait and when we heard a favorable weather report on the radio, Bud took off for Fairbanks. He needed to get back in time to fly fishermen in to the lodge. Later in August he was scheduled to fly in some resident hunters.

He loaded up, kissed us goodbye, shoved the little plane into the wind, spun the prop and taxied off and was soon airborne, waggling his wings in farewell. An hour later the lake was calm with the sun shining and warm.

That evening came a message to me via Tundra Topics: "Bud Conkle arrived safely in Fairbanks today at six o'clock after fighting headwinds all the way from Tanada Lake."

His flight to Fairbanks took five and a half hours. Normally it took three hours, but he had headwinds all the way and had to land twice to gas up. He had left Tanada with full tanks plus ten gallons of aviation gas in 5-gallon cans. He barely made it to Harding Lake, 50 miles from Fairbanks, and had to land and borrow gas from the pilot of an Army plane parked there. While this was a long flight, I couldn't help but think of the contrast; previous trips from Tanada Lake to Fairbanks, including our hike out, had sometimes taken days.

All day I had worried, with visions of an accident. How would I know if Bud's plane went down? How long should I stay at Tanada Lake before hiking out to the road with the baby on my back? I cannot recount the number of times over the years that I had such worries. In September of that same year, for example, Bud flew to get the mail on what should have been a one day trip. Three days later, when he still hadn't returned, I was sure I was a widow with a little boy to raise. I readied myself for the long hike out to the road. I left a note in the cabin, and had started off when, miraculously, here came Bud in the little yellow Cub.

Eventually, of course, I realized that such worrying was a waste of time and energy, and I largely got over it. I had great confidence in Bud's ability to handle emergencies.

Late in the afternoon of the third day that Bud was gone I heard the distant drone of a familiar-sounding engine. I ran out to look, and there, against the far hillside, just under the low-hanging fog, was a moving bright yellow splash of color—our Cub. Bud circled, then glided in to land on the choppy water. The airplane was like a bird coming home to roost. Bud was tired and happy to be home. The load he carried was almost unbelievable. It didn't seem possible that it all could fit into that tiny airplane. There were cases of canned goods and milk, everything from our shopping list, plus a small Yukon stove—which in turn was filled with loose items. Too there was a 5-gallon can Bud had emptied into the plane when he had landed on a lake to gas up. I could see no room for the can in the rear and I suspect he carried it on his lap, although he wouldn't say.

On his return flight Bud had a harrowing flight through Isabel Pass in the Alaska Range. He had a tailwind, but updrafts and downdrafts bounced the Cub so much he feared the wings would come off. Flying close to the side of the pass, he tried for altitude to clear jagged rocks. Winds were so strong he expected any minute to be flung against a cliff. A terrific jolt caused the plane to shudder, and he told himself, "This is it for sure." Suddenly an updraft picked the plane up and flung it high, and then he was through the pass. When he reached Meier's Lake he landed to relax before gassing up for the rest of the flight home.

The Weasel and the Cub airplane replaced our dog team. Much as we loved our dogs we had to be practical. It was heart-wrenching to see them go. Friends at Fairbanks were happy to have good-natured, friendly Wooley for a pet. Smoke Thomas was glad to add such a good work dog as Black Boy to his team. Jim went to dog heaven where there are no more sleds to pull and no more cold winter nights

Tanada Lake Lodge.

curled up in a dog house. He was too crippled with arthritis or rheumatism to tolerate another winter, and we were too attached to him to send him to another home where he might not be well cared for. It was the kind thing to do, and I suspect he knew too when Bud led him away that it was to be a one-way trip for him. It was sad when Bud returned with Jim's chain and collar and no Jim. All he had ever known was the important job of leader of teams. Although it hurt his feelings to be second in command, he did a fine job of helping Bud train Keno to be a leader. Jim was quick to go gee or haw, and quick to nip Keno if he let slack in the tow line. Keno, of course, was our pet and so much a part of the family that he remained with us.

We had had our trials and tribulations—and our fun—with our dog team, but it was time for us to get on and work further toward the goal we had set for ourselves.

## XVI

## SEARCHING FOR SHEEP

A year had passed since we had started entertaining clients at our lodge. During the second summer Bud was kept busy ferrying fishermen to Tanada lake, and I was busy cooking and helping to entertain them. Bud had a number of hunts booked for the fall. The pure white wild sheep of Alaska's mountains—the Dall sheep—is considered by some sportsmen to be North America's finest big game trophy. Tanada Lake, in the foothills of the great Wrangell Mountains where live some of the finest and largest of Alaska's Dall sheep, was a jump-off point for hunts for these lovely animals. Bud quickly realized that he must find places where he could take his clients to hunt these sheep.

Thus in late July, 1953, we loaded our J-3 Cub with camp gear, filed a flight plan with a bush pilot friend, and roared across Tanada Lake and headed into the high Wrangells, bound for a small remote lake that Bud had discovered. We were to camp near the lake and scout nearby peaks for Dall rams. If we found them, Bud planned to establish a main hunting camp beside the little lake.

Two hours after we left Tanada Lake Bud circled the tiny high altitude lake. We lost altitude, skimmed just above treetops, and then Bud nosed the plane into the wind and side-slipped easily onto the choppy water. A wind spattered the lake with whitecaps. The ship wanted to weathercock as Bud taxied toward a favorable-looking anchorage. He had to use a lot of power, increasing the danger of hitting a

Tanada Lake in winter.

Tundra near Tanada Lake.

submerged rock and damaging one of the thin-walled floats. A grassy swamp proved to be a wise choice, and soon Bud had the floats pulled back as close to shore as the load in the plane permitted.

Bud's hip boots had been left behind as a weight-saving gesture. Barefooted, he carried 22-month-old Colin, then me, and finally the camp gear to a dry mound some distance across the low swamp. Then he lifted the rear end of the floats and pulled the lightened plane ashore, leaving its nose pointed into the wind where he tied it securely to sturdy scrub willows. While he was doing this I snuggled Colin into his daddy's flight jacket and he settled himself into the roomy canvas bag of my packboard, his little fists gripping the round railing across the top. In his short life Colin had learned to be as much at home in a packboard as most babies are in buggies on paved sidewalks.

Bud lifted this lively 25-pound cargo and held it while I got it comfortably on my back and adjusted the straps. Then with a much heavier pack on his back and .30–06 rifle in hand, he led the way into the dense spruce forest.

It was wonderful fun moving quietly through the thick woods with deep damp moss that cushioned our footsteps as we watched hopefully for signs of game. We knew we might see a moose or a grizzly bear. Bud's low whistle or a raised hand was my signal to stand motionless while he investigated something ahead. Colin, as young as he was, seemed to fall naturally into our pattern of behavior when we were on such jaunts.

Our destination was the base of a jagged range of lofty windswept peaks beyond the gently rolling green hills. Bud felt certain that the high hidden meadows of this range would pasture the great white sheep. We stalked through the heavy timber for half an hour, skirting the base of a low hill. Then we emerged into the open and dropped onto a wide gravel bar. A clear icy stream gurgled along its rocky channel from the canyon we planned to enter. All three of us walked beside the stream, moving leisurely, watching the moving water and the color variations in the rocks. Occasionally I grabbed the baby when his darting feet took him too close to the stream.

We entered the narrow canyon between high cut banks and crossed and recrossed the shallow stream many times in the next mile before its bed broadened, and we came within view of lovely sloping meadows. The sun shone softly on the broad side of a prodigious mountain that appeared to be no more than five miles away. Huge slides has scarred its sides, and windswept spots exposed a myriad of colors that glinted in the sun.

Soon dark clouds hid the sun and a drizzle started; then came rain. Beguiled by the lovely weather when we had left the airplane, I had packed rain gear in the bottom of Bud's pack. Now Bud decided to go ahead, find a sheltered spot, and make camp.

Colin enjoyed himself. Even in the heavy rain with a chilly wind blowing down the canyon he chattered happily. Huddled deep in the pack, snug in his favorite cap—a waterproof poplin of his daddy's that I had cut down to fit him—with the fur collar of Bud's flight jacket buttoned tightly around his neck, he stayed warm and dry.

Bud disappeared far ahead. As I crossed and recrossed the stream my leather-booted feet soon became soaking wet. The sociable companion on my back made it necessary for me to watch my footing and move steadily, rather than stop and gaze at the hills and daydream as I was inclined to do.

I finally rounded the sharp sheer rock bluff I had used as a landmark since losing sight of Bud. The exquisite odor of willow smoke drifted toward me from a cozy camp on a low grassy bank. We huddled around the fire for a time, and then the rain suddenly ceased. Soon all the tent ropes and willow branches in the vicinity of the fire were laden with drying clothes. We ate fried potatoes, beans with ham, cold biscuits with jelly, and cups of steaming tea.

A mile or so beyond us the wide gravel bar met the base of the colored mountain of the many slides and turned abruptly right, entering a narrow valley with the colored mountain on the far side and a steep, higher range on the other, its boulder-strewn summits and jutting peaks outlined against the clearing sky. The serrated peaks of a still higher range rose beyond. Across the bar to our left and beyond a sloping plateau we could see the mouth of a deep ragged ravine that led up into the higher levels of the colored mountain. Down a narrower steep gorge from the rocky heights of the colored mountain gushed a stream to join the smaller creek from the canyon to our right.

Where to explore? Bud glassed the high slopes and likely peaks in front of us and could see no sheep or their trails. We decided to leave camp where it was and hike as far as practicable into the canyon to our right. We were about seven miles from the plane, and Bud, thinking of the time factor and poor endurance of most nonresident hunters, didn't want to base camp too far from the lake where we had landed. We left all but rifle, camera, and binoculars in camp.

Near the entrance to the canyon we rounded a bend so sharp that it sent the waters of the creek rushing headlong against a high gravel bank. Here we stood fascinated by a beckoning vista. We estimated the canyon ran five miles to the base of the jagged range that seemed to reach above all the others.

After an hour of easy hiking Bud left Colin and me to rest beside a willow fire. We were about four miles from camp, but seemed to be no closer to the end of the canyon. Bud went to investigate what appeared to be a low pass to our right; it seemed possible that we could climb over the pass, drop into a canyon on the far side, cross a series of low hills, and arrive near our camp. If so we could see a lot of country without retracing steps.

Colin and I walked around one more bend of the river, up one more unexplored canyon, rounded the end of the next ridge—we were never satisfied. There was always more to see—something beyond this bend, or on the other side of that pass. This was the lure, the challenge that fascinated, the feeling that Bud and I had felt in common since first we met. We had chased unknowns together with great excitement since breaking free of the tenacious grip of city life. Colin, as young as he was, seemed to share our urgent desire to see and to know what was around that next bend, over the next hill.

Bud returned, having found an ideal site for an overnight

camp. We accompanied him to it, and Colin helped me gather dead willows and driftwood while Bud went back for our camp gear and tent. We tired of wood gathering and lay on the dry and warm moss, gazing at billowing white clouds. Ground squirrels and whistling marmots squealed warnings or made inquiries from their many vantage points around us.

Soon Bud was back and pitched our two-man tent and had a fire crackling nearby. We sat by the fire after supper, watching the shadows of the peaks lengthen, and wondered if the smoke of any other white man's fire had ever risen in these remote canyons. On my next trip for firewood I found evidence of another fire. Had it been an Indian? A white prospector? A hunter? A rusty milk can nearby appeared to me to have been used for target practice. "No," Bud said, after a glance. "Those holes were made by the teeth of a bear or a wolverine."

We came upon a mystery that is still unsolved in my mind. On the grassy shoulder of a gentle slope, far from any old slide path, we found about two dozen conical mounds of sand within a radius of about 50 feet. Three of the mounds were sprouting weeds and willows, but some looked newly formed. The highest was at least 20 feet tall, the lowest about ten feet. We searched for evidence of old placer digging, but could find nothing to indicate that the strange mounds were man-made.

Dark clouds gathered and under a cold unfriendly sky and an icy drizzle we crawled into our sleeping bags inside the tiny tent. We awoke to a steady pour of rain instead of the sunshine we had fervently hoped for. No matter how comfortable a down sleeping bag feels, come daylight and time to be about there comes a time when even the drenching rain outside the tent is more inviting than trying to find a comfortable spot on what has come to feel like a rock pile. On that morning the two-man tent was dripping inside, as waterproof tents usually do after a night's use.

Bud crawled out first and tried to wriggle into his clothes without touching the wet ceiling. With uncomplimentary remarks about the weather in general and waterproof tents in particular, he crawled out of the mosquito-net-covered hole which served as a door. Shortly his cheerful whistling and the beautiful sound of a crackling campfire lured me out. Colin lay sleeping peacefully, looking tiny even in the narrow bed. I emerged wearing waterproof jacket and Bud's old rain pants.

No sooner had I settled comfortably by the fire with a cup of fragrant coffee than a wee red head peeped out of the tent opening. Bright blue eyes sized up the layout, then, bare-footed, his plastic night panties billowing like a balloon, Colin streaked over to cuddle in my lap. No sissy hovering and shivering for him!

The rain eased, then stopped. Enough sun peeked through the overcast to set us hurriedly packing. I dressed Colin warmly and settled him into my packboard for his daddy to carry. We piled things we didn't take with us inside the tent and set off with lunch, camera, rifle, binoculars.

Nearing the foot of a shale slide Bud's trained eye found the bleached skull and massive horns of a long-dead sheep. The curl had been a good 44 inches (measured around the curve), huge for a Dall sheep. Evidence pointed to wolves as cause of the ram's death. Where there was one, were there others? We hurried on with new enthusiasm.

We climbed, and were soon crossing loose shale slides. Bud soon outdistanced me, maneuvering across every-widening slide paths with that precious cargo riding with full confidence on his back. My knees began to feel shaky, my feet slipped on the smooth rocks, and when a rock gave way under my feet to roll far down the steep slope, I wondered how soon it would be before I joined it.

A drizzling rain started, making the rocks slippery. At long last Bud sat on a mossy ledge. Breathless, I reached the ledge to "set a spell" too. With binoculars, despite the misty rain and wet lense I saw three bull caribou grazing on the green slope on a far hillside. Their gray coats were sleek, and each carried impressively large antlers, bulging with dark velvet.

Taking turns with the glasses, we watched the three bulls bed down near the center of a long sloping hill where they could see in all directions. Rested, we moved on. I became greatly concerned over the steep and rough going I could see ahead, and I was even more scared at the idea of returning the way we had come. For the fifth or maybe the fiftieth time I told myself, "Never again will I climb in sheep mountains with Bud Conkle!" I never knew where he was going, how far he was going, or whether we would ever get back. Somehow I easily forgot when another season rolled around and I had the opportunity to accompany him.

I thought back to my first sheep hunt with my newly licensed guide-husband. I was to shoot the first ram. Pretending a courage I did not have, I crossed the inevitable shale slides, knees shaking and cold sweat on my brow. On one particularly bad slide I looked down and saw only gray shale clear to the canyon floor a thousand feet below. A slight disturbance could have caused an avalanche, gathering momentum and volume all the way to the canyon floor. I had a fleeting vision of being caught in such a slide. At just that moment rocks began to move under my feet. Petrified, I just stood there. A sharp command from Bud a few yards ahead and already off the slide spurred me to action and I quickly crossed to safety.

By the time we had reached the top of the highest mountain I had ever climbed, then crawled within 300 yards of the ram we sought, I was too winded to shoot. I begged off. "I might miss at this range, and then we'll have to chase him over another mountain."

Bud's .30–06 spoke, and the ram fell without ever knowing he had company on the mountain.

It was out of question to carry the sheep meat back down the way we had come up. Bud scouted and found a sheep trail down a fairly easy descent. Easy, if one could keep balanced, and run down a steeply sloping hillside across soft dirt and shale slides. I don't know how a man of so slight a build as Bud's could carry heavy loads on his back and still keep his balance. He had nearly 100 pounds of meat in his pack, with the heavy horns lashed on top. I carried both rifle, and in my pack were the heart and liver, and a few small chunks of meat. Bud, balancing the unwieldy load, raced along with the ease of a mountain goat, climbing over boulders and trotting along narrow ledges.

Not me. A hundred times I was sure I would lose my

198

An exceptional caribou.

balance, and once I did. Luckily it was not in one of those dangerous places with nothing to cling to, nothing to get a foothold in for a thousand feet straight down. I rolled a few feet and came to rest against a boulder, and both rifles survived undamaged. I vowed then that if ever I was tempted to go on another sheep hunt, I'd sit by the fire in camp while others did the climbing and hunting.

I wasn't invited to go on a sheep hunt the following year. Colin was ten months old when another season rolled around and I went as cook while Bud and three friends sought rams from a base camp seven miles from Tanada Lake. That season I did stay in camp—chasing the baby most of the time.

Now here I was again on a mountain of bare tumbled rock, in a cold drizzling rain to boot, and with the baby along. I must have been mad.

We soon gained the base of a flat-sided boulder which jutted from the hill and obstructed our view. Below was a deep gully. It appeared impossible for us to go farther in that direction, but at the very edge of the steep drop into the gully Bud found almost perfect stepping stones around the flat face of the boulder. They led to irregular but solid rock footing. We easily climbed a rocky ledge, and we found good walking over a low saddle onto an adjoining hill.

Finally we stood drinking in a breath-taking panorama. We could see countless miles in all directions. There were bare inaccessible peaks to the northeast, a full sweep of jagged mountains behind us, gently rolling mossy hills below, and beyond them a range of desolate peaks we had not previously seen. A series of fault-topped ridges led from the hill on which we stood, with a wide flowing valley on either side. Each ridge connected with a slightly higher ridge until they came to a knife-sharp ridge that sloped up to higher levels of those bleak and barren peaks.

I stood spellbound, thankful I had found the stamina to make the climb. Bud and Colin sat side-by-side, glassing the hills in all directions. The drizzle had stopped, but low fog enveloped most of the peaks and hung in all the low pockets, hiding places where sheep should have been.

We saw no game, put Colin back in the pack, and crossed

a connecting saddle to the next hill and had a better look into a high draw. A moving object appeared on the horizon behind me, and Bud had gone on. The object was too tall and slender for me to identify. I caught up with Bud, got binoculars, and ran back around the hill to inspect this thing. What I had mistaken for a large creature of some kind turned out to be two hoary marmots. They were much larger than any I had ever seen, and they stood and acted together, bobbing as one to have a better look at me, and, still in unison, sat down again. I enjoyed watching their antics, but Bud urged me along. He had spotted something white on a far hillside.

He had found a small band of ewes and lambs grazing contentedly in a meadow across a wide canyon. We watched them for a time, enjoying the peaceful pastoral scene. We had scanned hundreds of square miles of what looked like marvelous sheep range, but we had found no rams, the object of our search.

It grew late and Bud wanted to get to the next ridge. He left Colin and the rifle with me and headed out on what I considered a high lope, leaving instructions about where we were to wait for him. While he climbed, Colin and I went down the gentle slope to the canyon floor. We reached an open gravel bar near a creek, gathered willows, and built a fire and rested. Shortly Bud arrived. He had seen no rams.

Cold wind and chilling rain swept down the canyon, at our backs this time. Bud outdistanced me, and when finally I arrived in camp he had a crackling fire burning, and Colin was sitting in its welcome heat, a big raincoat propped over his back.

The clouds broke and stray beams of afternoon sunlight came to lift our spirits. Bright-eyed parka squirrels darted into camp to sample food we had out while we quietly sat watching them. Shy at first, they would run toward us, sit up to look questioningly, then dart back to what they thought was a safe distance. Two or three of the boldest popped saucy heads into our food containers and scampered off with full mouths.

On the third morning lead-gray skies greeted us when we poked heads out of the tent. Ominous clouds gathering in the direction of the plane gave us an uneasy feeling. We knew from experience that violent summer storms are likely to last three or four days, and we didn't want to spent that time waiting out the weather if we could help it. We hurried breakfast and headed for the airplane. A dismal rain pelted us the full five miles back down the canyon.

We rounded a bend, then stopped to rest and have a last look at the slide-scarred colored mountain in the distance. A few slanting rays of the sun leaked through the overcast and turned the entire mountainside into enchanting loveliness. A slight movement attracted us and we turned to watch a bull caribou with a snow white neck and a magnificent set of antlers emerge from a ravine and run up a slope. He halted for a moment, then ran nervously to the shoulder of a plateau to stand and sniff the air. He had apparently heard our voices, but was unable to catch our scent. Moments later he loped gracefully into a draw and out of sight.

When it was my turn with the binoculars two rams grazed into view on distant steep rocky cliffs, their white coats glistening, and when rays of the sun struck them for a fleeting moment they stood out like fluorescent lights against the dark-shadowed background.

Bud lay on his stomach for a long while, studying the rams through the glasses. "Small, both of them," he finally announced. Although there might be larger rams back in the canyon, there was nothing to warrant his setting up a sheep hunting camp here. He knew of other places where there were more rams, some with big heads.

While we were intent on studying the sheep, Colin climbed the nearby hillside and was nearly to the top before I missed him. I got my exercise going after him, for when he saw me coming he went farther and faster. I should have sent his daddy.

Colin bubbled over with chatter as we neared the tiny lake that held our Cub, and two bull moose left off browsing to bolt into the forest. We caught a glimpse of their huge antlers before they blended with the shadows.

At the lake a stiff breeze was blowing, enabling Bud to lift the plane off with us and all our camp gear: he had expected to have to leave the gear behind and make a second trip. As we climbed into the mountain air the hills of home were shining clear and inviting on the horizon. The waters of Tanada Lake were tranquil as our floats touched and we skimmed to our anchorage near our green-roofed cabin. Our little yellow bird had again brought us safely home.

# XVII

## SHEEP, BEARS, AND WOLVES

It was almost a foregone conclusion that Colin would shoot a Dall ram before I did. And he did. He was twelve, and we called it the "Before Breakfast Ram."

We were in a spike camp in the sheep hills above Tanada Lake, camped on, of course, Sheep Lake. Bud had left camp to fly our nonresident hunter-client to another camp, for the man had collected his ram. Colin and I were in camp with Herb, an assistant guide. Herb was up at daylight to put the coffee on, but he no more than had the fire going when I heard him call, "Colin, get dressed and let's go get this big ram. It's feeding up the hillside in plain sight and may not stay around long."

I sat in camp and watched. Through binoculars I saw the two hunters now and then from behind boulders and brush as they made the stalk after climbing above the still-feeding ram. I couldn't judge the distance Colin was shooting from, but the first shot, with his dad's .30–06 rifle, hit a rock just under the ram. The surprised animal turned to look when the second shot splattered rocks at its feet. That was when it decided to leave the area. The third shot rang out and the bullet hit that ram right in the ear as it bounded uphill. It fell, instantly dead.

"Colin, how come you couldn't hit it when it wasn't running?" Herb asked.

While they skinned and butchered I climbed up to help pack some of the meat, and to be sure that the heart,

Two hunters, two sheep.

tongue, and liver were saved. Herb carried the heaviest load and Colin wanted to carry his own trophy sheep horns, and it was a fine trophy, too, with 39 inches around the curl, and 14-inch circumference at both bases. Colin tied the horns high on his pack along with all the meat a slightly-built twelve-year-old could stagger downhill with. I followed. Colin tried to jump a narrow deep creek and because of the overbalanced pack, he fell short. The horns were just wide enough that they hung up on the brush on the bank. The pack slid forward, pushing Colin's head down almost into the water. He lay in this embarrassing position with his feet kicking in the air. His language at that moment included words gleaned from some of the choicest of his dad's vocabulary—words that neither used often, especially within my earshot. I found his predicament a bit on the humorous side, and I'm afraid I was a bit slow in helping him regain his feet. I had a feeling that he had been walking along thinking of himself as a world-class big game hunter. He was eager to be back on his feet before Herb returned and found him in that undignified posture.

My sheep hunt came a couple of years later. We were again camped on Sheep Lake, with friends. Colin was to be my guide. Bud had hired a cook (other than me!) and I had a week's vacation without pay. We had climbed to a 3,000-foot elevation meadow where four trophy rams were feeding. Two appeared to have identical size horns. It was a lovely fall day in late August, and the view from the heights was well worth the climb. Our tents looked like miniatures in the distance, with the blue Piper Super Cub of our friend tied close. The air was pure and clean, enabling us to see great distances. I love camping in a tent at the base of high mountains. Evenings by a comfortable campfire watching a harvest moon emerge from behind nearby peaks, sharing pleasures with friends and son, make for unforgettable moments.

I missed the 40-inch ram at 75 yards. He was a beautiful sight standing by a rock. I had the crosshairs of the scope of the accurate .270 rifle on him when I fired—or so I thought. No matter. I had the satisfaction of seeing that great wild ram in the crosshairs of a rifle that could easily have ended his existence. My bullet went high, and missed cleanly. The ram exploded into action, and left without giving me a second chance or a thank you that he was alive and unhurt.

His grazing companions also left in a shower of rocks and flying feet, and also without a backward glance to see if I was a threat to their lives. I was elated, knowing my ram had his freedom and would continue to roam those high peaks. I like to see animals in the wild, preferring them there to hanging on a wall. Besides, that ram was bigger than the one that Bud shot and had mounted, and now I could point out that I had missed a bigger ram than the one he had shot. Colin's 39-inch ram horns made a nice mount, and were hung on a plaque on our trophy room wall beside those of the same size his dad had shot.

Clearly, I am not a dedicated hunter. Many times I have wished I had more courage as a hunter, especially during occasional encounters with grizzly bears. Over the years we had problems with various grizzlies. I don't remember how many messes I had to clean up after a bear got into a cabin and tore it up. We expected this, for we moved into bear territory when we established Tanada Lake Lodge. To avoid bear problems, we did our best to keep temptation out of their way. I didn't mind so much cleaning up messes made by bears in our cabins as I did the messes left by hippies who used the trailer we kept parked near the highway. We housed our hunters in the trailer when we moved them back and forth to various hunting camps. Hippies even got into and made a mess of our Rufus Creek cabin, after stealing everything worth anything, and burning all the firewood and kindling and not replacing it.

Most bears go about their own business and don't bother things if they are only passing through. Of the two animals, the hippy types, who sometimes call themselves hunters, are the more destructive.

Many years after Tanada Lake Lodge was established and running, Bud and I homesteaded some land on the Tok Highway not far from the lodge. We needed a place for the horses we started using for our big game hunts, and it was more convenient to spend winters at the homestead near the highway. Early one winter morning when we were at the homestead I was first up and looked out the bedroom window and saw a grizzly bear on its hind legs reaching for a cache where we had put our frozen Christmas turkey. It was time for bears to be in hibernation, not out raiding our cache.

I wanted Bud to see that bear, thinking he might have seen it while flying. Also, I wanted to avoid his, "Oh, it just looked big to you because you can't judge their size!"

"Come quick. A grizzly is after our turkey!" I said. Not exactly the words a peacefully sleeping man wants to hear. The bear was sniffing back and forth, with his nose pressed against the screening, savoring the good smell.

"Hey you, get the hell out of there," Bud, in pajamas, yelled as he opened the window.

I thought that surprised bear was going to jump clear over the cache. As it was, he bumped against it and knocked it over, rolled over sideways, gained his feet and for many minutes we heard him crashing through trees and brush. He never did return. I always enjoyed looking at bear's backends as they departed.

This approach didn't work a year later on another grizzly. That bear was standing up trying to tear out the rear window of our new Chrysler station wagon where it was parked beside our cabin. We had arrived late from hunting and had left two hind quarters of moose in the Chrysler. Bud had awakened during the blackest part of the night, thinking from all the scratching that our two cats were up to something.

He opened the bedroom window when he saw the bear and yelled, "Hey you, get the hell out of there," expecting the bear to depart as had the previous one. Instead this bear dropped to all fours and came at Bud, whacking the side of the cabin as Bud slammed the window shut.

"That bear is dangerous and has to go," Bud growled as he groped in the dark for a light.

"Where's the flashlight? LeNora, get up and get a light so I can find the shells for my rifle."

The rifle had been unloaded when we put it in the

Hunters heading out at Tanada Lake.

Chrysler for the drive home, and now it was in another room of the house. But where were its shells? Probably in the car, with the big flashlight, I guessed silently.

That was a night of confusion and unpreparedness.

"The lantern is empty, and I can't find my flashlight," was my excited response. "Where did you put the Blazo? I can't find it."

"Why didn't you fill it before we left? That bear isn't going to give up. He's after that moose meat, and we've got to do something, quick," Bud muttered. He was in the next room with a lighted match, looking through a box of groceries we had brought inside. Maybe the rifle shells were there.

The matchlight revealed a flashlight under the bed, beyond easy reach, where a happy-to-see-us cat had knocked it. When Bud shined the light out the window the bear was still next to the Chrysler looking frustrated. When the light hit him he growled.

Bud finally found shells for the .375 rifle that he used for back-up when guiding bear hunters. I found the Blazo and filled the lantern with shaking hands, then lit it. Then it was my job to hold the light at the rear door while Bud handled the bear. I opened the door and cautiously stepped out, holding the lantern high, and the bear took off into the darkness. Bud shot into the air a couple of times, the loud booms of the heavy rifle shattering the still night. We waited. No sign of the bear. Bud handed me the rifle and went to the Chrysler to get the other rifle and lantern and a larger flashlight. The bear emerged from the opposite end of the cabin just as Bud reached the front door of the Chrysler. I could see Bud, but I couldn't see the bear, but by the way Bud hollered and cussed I thought the bear was after him. I couldn't shoot because I was afraid of hitting Bud.

Bud and the bear looked at each other, and Bud stood his ground and bluffed the bear, but said later he would have had time to jump in the car if the bear had come any closer. Apparently the bear was as surprised to see Bud as Bud was to see the bear, and again it disappeared into the darkness.

We had the distinct impression that the bear wasn't going to discourage easily. Bud vividly remembered it slamming into the cabin next to the window after he had yelled at it. We put the tempting moose meat away in a freezer, and for the balance of the night we were prepared for its return. Happily, it didn't come back.

I was alone at Tanada Lake one late afternoon when I happened to look back over my shoulder in time to see a grizzly loping down the trail toward me, and not as far away as I prefer grizzlies. I have often since wondered how I'd have fared if I hadn't seen that bear when I did. Was it instinct or training to always be alert? I don't remember hearing anything to cause me to turn and look. I think it took me no more than three long jumps to reach the door of the guest cabin I was near. Under other circumstances it would have taken me three times that many.

With hand on doorknob I turned to look back. The bear was sniffing the ground I had recently vacated. It wasn't an awfully big bear, but Bud always said that any bear was big enough to tear an arm or a leg off if it had a mind to. Wearing a buckskin jacket, I had been leaning over to examine a fresh cow moose track, trying to figure out where she had appeared from so abruptly. She had suddenly materialized in front of me, hackles up, as I hung a sheet blanket on a clothesline I had stretched across the trail. I thought the moose was going to charge me, and the only thing I could think to do was to shake the blanket in her face and yell. This turned her, and she leaped the nearby berm, and as she did I saw a tiny reddish calf at her side.

I am convinced the bear was after the calf, and the cow was fleeing the bear when she came upon me blocking her trail.

With my buckskin jacket, and leaning over, the grizzly could easily have mistaken me for the calf, and I have always wondered about it.

I got a rifle from the cabin and shot in the air in the direction of the bear. It leaped the berm, going the direction the cow and calf had taken. As I stood there listening, shook up from nearly being charged by a cow moose and a grizzly bear all within moments, the bear peeked at me from behind the outhouse, probably wondering who I was to interfere in its chase of moose. I shot again fairly close

A happy moose hunter.

Dinner for an entire camp.

above its peeking head, and I heard it leave, crashing through the brush up through the timber.

Next day the cow and her tiny calf were in our yard browsing, so I knew the calf hadn't ended up on the grizzly's dinner menu.

One early March day Bud was flying near the headwaters of the Copper River when he saw two big gray wolves traveling together. He had a permit to shoot wolves from the air (they were issued by the Fish and Wildlife Service to anyone who wanted one during Territorial days), but he was unable to maneuver them into a place where he could shoot from the air and also land to retrieve, so he let them go.

He flew back across Copper Lake, heading home, when he came upon an unusual wilderness drama—a wolverine attempting to catch caribou. Snow was deep, and the wolverine was having a hard time. It scratched snow three feet into the air with almost every bound as it vainly tried to catch a swiftly running caribou. The caribou easily outdistanced the wolverine, and it gave up the chase, retraced its trail and started after another member of the herd that had stood watching the first attempt. The caribou that had outdistanced the wolverine returned to stand with the others and watch. After the third caribou outdistanced the short-legged wolverine it gave up and wandered off. Although the wolverine had appeared determined, the caribou didn't seem to take it very seriously. Bud had to give the wolverine credit for trying.

Bud was experienced in aerial shooting of wolves by this time. When he first started seeking wolves with the plane and took a shotgun and a box of buckshot with him when he went to Slana for mail, I told him, "I sure would feel more at ease if I knew you had practiced shooting out of the airplane while flying alone."

"What better practice than shooting at a live wolf?" he had countered. "Experience comes from inexperience." He didn't fool me a bit. It was always a worry for the families of aerial wolf-hunters when they left, wondering whether the pilot or the wolf would win. The wolf won more than once over the years, as aerial wolf hunting caused many airplane crashes, and not a few pilots and gunners were killed.

He was to get much experience that winter flying and shooting at wolves by himself. Then he managed to shoot himself down:

He was half way across six-mile long Copper Lake when a large black wolf ran out from the timbered shore directly ahead of the J-3 Cub. The control for the Cub was a stick, not a wheel. While shooting Bud had learned how to hold the stick steady between his knees. When he saw the black wolf he opened the right door and throttled back to fly in low over the running animal. He pointed his double-barreled Winchester shotgun at the predator, but the wolf seemed unaware of the airplane, and it was holding to its course, and it seemed to Bud that he could get closer.

"End of the trail for you, old boy," Bud thought. Just then a gust of wind hit the plane, slamming the shotgun barrel against the fuselage, causing the gun to fire. The instant vibration of the Cub told Bud that he had accomplished what he had hoped would never happen—he had shot one tip off of the propeller. With several inches missing on one side, the propeller was out of balance, and it was impossible to remain airborne.

He cut the throttle and easily landed on the frozen lake. As soon as he stopped he leaped out with the shotgun and got off two shots at the fleeing wolf, which was now putting distance between itself and the big bird that had come out of nowhere. The distance was too great. It wasn't the end of the trail for that old wolf after all.

Bud had shot himself down about five miles from Tanada Lake. At the time we lived in a new cabin we had built at more distant Cobb Lake, but we still owned and operated Tanada Lake Lodge. The temperature was −20 F. when Bud put on the snowshoes he always carried tied to the lift strut. He dragged some heavy trees out to tie the plane to, and buried them in snow, then he snowshoed the five miles to Tanada. He removed a wooden souvenir propeller from the wall and with it hiked back to the airplane.

At the plane, with ten miles of hiking behind him, Bud removed the damaged propeller and put the wooden propeller on. The bolt holes lined up fine, but the wooden propeller was thicker than the metal one, and the bolts were too short. He needed to counter-sink the wooden prop to make the bolts fit.

"Now why didn't I think of that while I was at the cabin where all my tools are," he said, shaking his head.

Tired and exasperated he returned to Tanada in the dark, completing fifteen miles of hiking. It took some time before he got the cold cabin sufficiently warm to go to bed. He had four hours of sleep and no breakfast, then hiked the five miles back to the Cub. The trail he had broken was solid now, so he didn't need to wear snowshoes. Working on the ice of the lake it was a cold, finger-freezing job counter-sinking holes in the wooden propeller. It had to fit snugly, with no play.

Bud didn't like the idea of anyone having to rescue him, and he always requested that I give him time to walk out if he was ever overdue with the airplane. This was one time that I hadn't paced the floor worrying. When he didn't arrive before dark I assumed he was at the Tanada Lake cabin.

He had to heat the Cub engine with the fire pot after replacing the propeller, so it was nearly noon before he flew over the cabin at Cobb Lake to let me know he was back. The substitute propeller gave the little yellow plane a different sound, and I had to look twice to be sure it was Bud who had buzzed the cabin. I had been thinking of trying to call Cleo McMahan to go look for Bud, and was relieved when he arrived.

A year later Bud shot a black wolf while aerial hunting on the open rolling hills above Copper Lake. When he skinned it he discovered two number 4 buckshot just under the hide. No doubt it was the same wolf that he had shot at, when instead he had shot the tip off of his propeller. The wolf was an unusually large old male with bad teeth. We had the hide made into a rug mount then hung it on the wall above the damaged propeller.

That shotgun-blasted propeller tip was instantly recognized for what it was by every pilot who saw it displayed on the wall of our trophy room. It elicited myriads of humorous comments and suggestions on how to and how-not-to

Dinner in Sheep camp.

hold a shotgun when shooting from an airplane. It was a real conversation piece for pilots who had hunted wolves from the air, and many of these pilots shared with us interesting experiences. Such pilots almost invariably suggested that the other tip of the propeller blade could have been shot off, and both filed smooth, so Bud could have flown the plane home. I wonder how many pilots did this?

It never ceased to amaze me that people who saw that black wolf skin thought it was a black bear. They apparently didn't realize that a bear doesn't have a long tail. Bud thought that his black wolf was probably quite happy with the admiration it received from many people over the years—happier than it would have been had it disappeared into oblivion as it would have if its fate had been left to Mother Nature.

I would like to think so.

## XVIII

## WIND ON THE WATER

Tanada means wind-on-the-water in the Athabascan language of the Nabesna (ice people) Indians. We had lived on the lake for several years when a young Native boy who grew up at Batzulnetas Village explained this to me. It fits.

The lake is up to 180 feet deep, six miles long, and is a mile wide at its widest point. The long axis lake lies in a north-south direction. A large bay of Tanada extends to within two miles of Copper Lake, a similar-sized lake to the west. Winds funneling down the valley between mountains to the south, or from across the bay from Copper Lake, may come up suddenly and whip the normally calm water of Tanada into three and four-foot waves. Once we started using the airplane for transportation we were more alert to the wind on the water, for parked airplanes are vulnerable to wind, and winds and high waves may keep an airplane from the air. Impatient pilots who put their planes down on Tanada Lake learned to wait—or they learned more about the limits of the airplanes they flew. Bud had a few names for the winds that scourged Tanada Lake, especially when he wanted to fly, but they aren't appropriate for a family journal.

A number of the local Indians have recounted legends of a monstrous fish that supposedly lived in Tanada Lake. It was reputed to be so huge that when it surfaced and slapped the water with its tail, it created a wave that washed the shore, and easily swamped any boat. One day this fish

Sheep hunting means climbing to high places.

slapped the water with its tail and swamped the boat in which a tribal chief was paddling. The boat overturned, and the chief drowned, and the people believed that the huge fish ate the chief, for the body was never found. The Natives from Batzulnetas Village sited on Copper River refused to again put a boat on Tanada Lake.

Twice in the 20 years we lived at Tanada Lake we saw what we like to think was the legendary fish. A lake trout seemingly as long as the fourteen-foot-long boat we were in once surfaced near, following the oversize Daredevl lure that Bud was trolling. Appearing suddenly, it gave us a real start. Both of us saw it. It refused the lure, nudged it briefly, and was gone.

Two years later in the same boat Bud saw a monster lake trout grab a ten-inch lake trout a lady angler had reeled to the surface. The huge fish gracefully surfaced without creating much more than a ripple on the surface, then it disappeared into the murky depths. The lady's reel spun out line as she tried to hold the monster, but her 6-pound line snapped. Bud tried every lure and every technique he knew to lure this eye-popper into again striking, but to no avail.

Tanada Creek's clear green water winds its way from the northern end of Tanada Lake to empty a few miles away into the silty Copper River. Decaying Indian fish wheels, designed for catching migrating salmon, reminded us of times gone by. Batzulnetas Village had been abandoned perhaps 20 years before we arrived, and only the village community hall, one of the many log cabins, and the high pole caches with doors ajar and roofs collapsing, remain standing in the overgrown willows. A patina of age had settled on the once-white-washed picket fences surrounding the graves. An epidemic—small pox or influenze—put many of the residents in these graves, and the survivors fled.

In the winter of 1794–95 Russian explorer-traders ascended the Copper River to buy furs and to kill the men and take women captives. Quite a number of Russians were killed at Batzulnetas, according to stories handed down by the Indians. (I found confirmation of this in a University of

Alaska publication, *The Headwaters People's Country*, by James Kari, Alaska Native Language Center, 1986.)

I treasure two old and unusual bowls with the Russian coat of arms embossed on them which Harry Boyden gave me. Presumably they were left by the Russians more than a century ago, when Alaska was a Russian colony. Another fascinating historic relic we found near the lake included remnants of double-ender freighting sleds that early in this century horses pulled past Tanada Lake and on through Pass Creek to the Nabesna Mine. A double-ender sled was built so that if the sled mired down, the horses could be hitched to the other end to pull it out.

We had our tragedies in building our Tanada Lake Lodge and the guiding business. On July 3, 1951, my cousin Harvey Steele drowned in Tanada Lake. We don't know how it happened. Harvey left the lodge in a boat heading for the lower end of the lake. In the boat with him was the repaired track of the Weasel. I watched Harvey as he headed across the lake, and until he was out of sight. Bud's last words to him were, "Cross the lake, then follow the shoreline." This was the safest course: if the boat sank near shore, presumably Harvey, a strong swimmer, could make shore.

High winds came up after Harvey left. Bud flew to the south end and waited, but dark came and Harvey didn't arrive. Bud then walked the shoreline and found the boat where it had washed ashore about halfway up the lake. The wind was blowing a gale. At daylight he repeatedly flew low over the entire shoreline of Tanada Lake. He found no trace of Harvey, then flew to notify the Troopers and Harvey's wife Hazel. Friends and neighbors came and searched, but no trace of Harvey was ever found—not even the blue cap he always wore.

The only explanation we could guess at was that high waves swamped the boat and the heavy track was dumped. Then the boat floated ashore. But why didn't Harvey cling to the boat? He was a strong swimmer. Perhaps he thought he could swim ashore, but the distance was too great and the water too cold. We will never know.

Tanada Lake isn't the only Alaskan lake with wind. A

year after Harvey drowned, our J-3 Cub needed new fabric. We expected fishing clients over the 4th of July, with other fishermen expected during the balance of July. In early June I drove to Fairbanks while Bud flew the Cub in, planning to complete the fabric work ourselves. We stayed with our bachelor friend Johnny Cross and worked on the airplane in his garage. Bud and an aircraft mechanic friend and I removed the old fabric, made a few minor repairs, and then I cut and fit the grade A fabric for fuselage and wings. All went well but the job took longer than expected, and of course it cost more than we anticipated.

The airplane was ready to fly by July 1, but Bud had to wait for a Civil Air Administration (predecessor to the FAA) inspector to approve the work and license the airplane. Colin and I left in the afternoon for the long drive home, leaving Bud on a slough of the Chena River awaiting the federal inspector.

Colin and I were driving merrily along nearly 100 miles from Fairbanks when we saw Bud standing beside the road waving us down. He had encountered strong headwinds and had landed the Cub on Boleo Lake, a few miles east of Big Delta and four or five miles from the Richardson Highway. Two U.S. Army float planes were tied to the dock, and it was all Bud could do to get the Cub safely on the water and tied to the dock beside the two other planes.

Soldiers on duty promised to watch the Cub, and he had rushed out to the highway to stop us if we hadn't already passed. We drove back to Boleo Lake and found our newly re-covered J-3 Cub lying on its back on the rocky beach. The soldiers had gone for coffee. In their absence a terrific gust had lifted the Cub out of the water, breaking the tie-down ropes, turning it upside down, and carrying it over the tops of both of the nearby Army planes.

If the Army lads hadn't been there sympathizing with us I am sure that Bud and I would have sat down and cried. The propeller and floats were undamaged. The engine required minor repair. But, sadly, the shiny red wings that I had sanded and polished to a glossy surface were crumpled and torn.

The soldiers helped Bud remove the wings. We tied the

fuselage to the pickup we were driving and towed it backwards to Fairbanks. Next day we retrieved the wings.

Jess Bachner, at Fairbanks Aircraft Service, agreed to do the repairs, and said we could pay when our hunting season was over. The Cub would be ready in two weeks. We drove home and waited for a message on Tundra Topics that the airplane was ready.

We did receive a $500 deposit for a 20-day fall hunt from our first nonresident big game hunter. It saved us. Upon our request for a loan our Fairbanks bank said, "Sorry. You're too far away from civilization. You'll never get enough business to be profitable."

Two years later that same bank willingly deposited a thousand dollars in our checking account when we telephoned from the Lower 48 states where we were visiting, no questions asked. "Just pay it back after hunting season." We also had good credit for groceries, car repairs, and aviation gas at Valdez.

The improvements came slowly. Two comfortable chairs and green linoleum on the floor. Oil cloth on the rough table that Bud built. Yellow curtains at the windows. With our white enamel cooking range, our little cabin had a homey atmosphere. I could comfortably seat eight fishermen and hunters at the table. Word-of-mouth spread the news that the Conkles produced good big game trophies; that there was fine fishing at Tanada Lake and on nearby lakes where Bud could fly; and that our lodge provided comfortable quarters and good food, and that Tanada Lake Lodge was a warm friendly place to visit.

There were beavers and muskrats in abundance in and around Tanada Lake where Bud could fly and land, so that when trapping season ended he had his limits of beaver, as well as nice catches of other furs. These brought a good price in Fairbanks. I was always glad when the trapping season ended with no more furry creatures in a box in the kitchen to thaw and return my looks when I glanced in their direction. I admit I was more than happy to spend the money their pelts brought, although for some years there was little left over after buying equipment and paying for repairs.

It was a big moose.

Bud kept busy building cabins, hauling supplies, and repairing outboard motors and other equipment when he wasn't flying. When things seemed a little boring, Colin provided some unwanted excitement. Bud, laying roofing paper on our new addition left the ladder leaning against the house and returning from a trip to get a drink of water, found his 18-month-old son on the roof. Another time he left the ladder leaning against a tree where he was installing a radio antenna; as soon as he turned his back he had to climb the tree to retrieve Colin. I soon learned to keep our active child in red coats or shirts so we could spot him quickly. One day I looked out a window just in time to see a red coat on a very little boy, followed by his faithful pup, running on the thin ice of the lake. He was supposed to be playing where his daddy was working and keeping an eye on him. Bud caught him just as he ran to the edge of open water. Another time Bud retrieved him from a headfirst fall into a pool of icy water. We began to think that that kid of ours had a charmed life.

Bud had three framed windows at Jack Lake that he wanted to fly to Tanada Lake. We waited until there was someone at the lodge to untie the door of the Cub and remove the windows so the pilot could get out too. I was elected to fly to Jack Lake with Bud. Once there, with Bud in the pilot's seat, I slid each window in at an angle behind him. Six inches of the windows was sticking out the side of the airplane so that the door wouldn't close. I tied the windows securely, then tied the door. It was then up to me to spin the propeller so Bud could fly to Tanada, unload, and return for me.

I hoped that the Cub would fly thus loaded as I bravely stood on a float to prop the engine into life. I intended to pull my arms back on the downward pull like I had always seen Bud do. However, with him yelling instructions from inside the plane, including, "Pull your hands back quick or the prop will cut them off," I began to loose confidence. Probably I wasn't pulling as hard as I should have.

First try and the engine didn't start. Second try, and third try, and it still wouldn't start. I could tell by his voice that Bud's patience was running out. I yelled back at him that if he'd just shut up and quit yelling instructions I'd get the prop spinning even if I did lose both hands. He must have thought I would do just that, so he insisted I untie the ropes, unload the windows, and let him out.

He then started the engine with the first spin of the propeller and got back into his seat with the engine running and that propeller spinning nearby while I re-loaded the windows, tied him and the windows in again, tied the door, and released the tie-rope anchoring the plane and watched him get airborne and fly out of sight.

In a short time I gave a sigh of relief when I saw the Cub returning. While airplane and Weasel transportation from the Nabesna Road to Tanada Lake were superior to a dog team, there were some penalties.

Bob Burkholder, a predator control agent for the U.S. Fish and Wildlife Service, always remained with us over-night when he was in our area. He worked a large area with the Super Cub he flew, and often spent many days on his field trips. He liked to watch our progress, and he was always a welcome visitor. Many a night we remained up late listening to his stories. He told us about a big wolf pack that had been killing a moose or a caribou every couple of nights, and he spent three days putting out poison to control them. During this work he roughed it, living outside in the cold. Then one day he saw an old trapper's cabin in fair condition where he landed. The cabin was crude, but it was more inviting than camping under a spruce tree. His supper over, he rolled out his sleeping bag on the top bunk and snuggled down for a good sleep. He was nearly asleep when the rusty door hinges squeaked, alerting him that he was getting company. The door opened inward, and the latch hadn't held because of frost heaves, and Bob hadn't felt it necessary to brace it. He had his flashlight in the bunk with him, and expected perhaps a porcupine had come into the cabin. Imagine his surprise when he turned the light on and saw a full grown grizzly bear sniffing about half way in the door. He had left his rifle leaning behind the door.

What to do?

With hardly a thought, he threw the flashlight at the bear, yelling "Vamoose," or something stronger. The flashlight

Bud and client after fishing at Copper Lake.

bounced and went out, and all was dark. The bear sounded as if he was tearing the door off the hinges, and Bob couldn't tell if the bear was inside with the door closed, or outside.

His next move, Bob said, if the bear was trapped inside, would have been to toss his unzipped sleeping bag over the bear if it hadn't left through the only window, and take his chances of grabbing his rifle on the way out. His final remark left us laughing. "Now if a cheechako had put himself in that situation there would have been an excuse. For me, I guess I'm hopeless or just lucky."

Bud opposed the use of poison for controlling wolves, as did most of the pilots who hunted wolves with their airplanes. Bud killed a wolf every now and then from the Cub, and the money we received from the pelt, plus the $50 bounty paid by the Territory, was important to us. The poisoning of wolves was not only repugnant, it decreased his opportunities of killing or trapping wolves. We knew it was Burkholders's job as a predator control agent for the federal government, and we never let this interfere with our friendship. After statehood (1959) the Alaska Department of Fish and Game halted the use of poison.

Some especially pleasant moments in the years I spent at Tanada Lake remain in my memory. There was a fall evening when the dishes were done, and baby Colin and I took the boat onto the lake. A lone loon gave a haunting call in the distance. The lake's surface shivered along the shoreline. I rowed in preference to running the motor, for I didn't want to break the peaceful silence. The muffled murmurings of ducks near shore told us we were disturbing their rest. Mr. Jones the cat raised his head from where he was curled on the seat beside me to stare intently toward the ducks, and a slight twitch of the tip of his tail gave away what he was thinking.

I hadn't seen the cat when we left the dock, but he swam out to the boat to go with us, which he would do if we left him behind. He is the only cat I ever had that would deliberately jump into the water and swim, and I carried a towel in the boat to dry him with. Again a lone loon cried from somewhere near a dark shore, its call sounding like a distressed human. There is something haunting and mystical about a loon's cry on a tranquil lake at night. We didn't travel far and we didn't do anything but look, listen, and enjoy on that short jaunt onto that lovely and peaceful lake, but it was a brief moment with vivid images that I still treasure.

## XIX

## EARLY STRUGGLES

Our early years were lean, and every dollar we took in was badly needed. Fishing customers arrived mostly on weekends from late June until early August when hunting season opened. Bud would take his two-man tent and sleep beside the airplane at Jack Lake near the Nabesna Road waiting patiently for clients who drove out from Fairbanks or Anchorage after leaving work. Often they arrived at midnight or later, but, of course, at that time of year it was light all night. Sometimes no one showed up.

One memorable night he flew to Jack Lake just before midnight for five fishermen. They had arrived early. A cold wind was blowing and they had a campfire burning brightly, and they had well fortified themselves against the cold from the generous supply of booze they had brought. What startled Bud was seeing them sitting beside the fire on five-gallon cans of aviation gas he had left hidden in the brush. Not only were the cans next to their campfire, the men were all happily smoking, not realizing the danger.

Time to fly them to Tanada, and Bud had the plane pulled back against the shore where it was necessary to take a long step from the uneven tundra to the end of the float, then take two more steps to climb in. It was one passenger at a time, of course, in the two-place Cub. The first passenger didn't make that long step from shore, and I was obliged to get out of bed and build up the fire and find some of Bud's dry clothes for him to change into. He was larger than Bud, and he had to use strings to hold open places together. He was cold sober after his cold-water dunking.

The five had planned to fish all night, but Bud fortified them with coffee and had them wait until morning when they were sober and weren't in danger of falling out of the boat. Those five were some of our best customers over the next few years. They got the message that Bud had little patience with clients who over-indulged in booze, and after that one episode they were always well behaved and much fun.

The responsive waters of Tanada and Copper Lakes consistently produced fine fishing, so our summer income from guest fishermen was a good part of our business.

Our first non-resident big game hunter, Fred Packer, from Martins Ferry, Ohio, was the kind of sportsman who made our business such a pleasure. He collected four fine trophies, a Dall ram, a grizzly bear, a caribou, and a moose. These trophies took first place in a display of North American trophy species in Ohio and adjacent states shortly after his hunt. He was a good reference for us over the years, and we booked a number of clients on his recommendations.

That same fall, Bob Holland, a young man from Rehobeth Beach, Delaware, who had written us for two years and wanted a grizzly bear trophy but couldn't afford a hunt, came and worked for us to help pay for his hunt. He arrived on the last hunt before bear season closed.

We had seen a fine big black grizzly that spring and summer, always high on a hillside or a long distance from the lake. Earlier hunters had sought it, but were unable to find it. Bob Holland was good help, and when time came for him to hunt he and Bud spent much time trying to locate the black grizzly. They saw it late one evening near a gut pile from an earlier moose kill and made an eight mile hike and overnighted close to the dense willows where they were sure it would be sleeping or feeding. Bud was so sure the bear was there that he had the hunter wait in the open, then he went into the thick willow brush to chase it out, guessing the direction the bear would run.

The black grizzly was there all right, but it outsmarted them, and ran out through thick willows toward the timber.

232

Neither of them saw it, but they heard it crashing as it left. When our young friend left that fall he took with him a trophy caribou in place of the black grizzly; that particular old griz had outsmarted all hunters that fall.

The following September the black grizzly was still wearing his glossy fur, and we hadn't seen him since summer, just prior to the opening of bear season. One day Bud flew to Jack Lake to pick up Bob Holland, who returned for another hunt. Collecting the black grizzly was his goal. On the way he saw the black grizzly feeding in a blueberry patch high on a hillside. It was in a perfect place for a stalk. Bud waited all afternoon and until dark, but Bob Holland didn't arrive. Two days later we received a message that he would be at Jack Lake to be picked up the next day; his delay had been caused by an accident he had had driving the Alcan Highway.

Again the two hunted the black grizzly for ten days, but the wise old bear couldn't be found. Instead, another grizzly hide went home with Bob Holland

During the following year we saw the black grizzly from time to time, sometimes when we glassed the hills, other times when we were flying. We grew fond of him. He never came near the cabin, nor threatened us. Bud was in hopes that he would continue to evade eager bear hunters, but it was not to be.

We were flying home one late afternoon on a cold winter day when all bears should have been in hibernation. As was Bud's habit upon returning to our cabin after an absence, he flew low over it and we could see that the door had been forced open. And there, running across the open tundra heading for timber, we saw the guilty party—the black grizzly.

We landed and cautiously approached the now-empty cabin. Fortunately for us the big bear hadn't been in the cabin long and damage was minimal. He had spilled sugar and flour on the floor, and some cans had been pulled off the shelves. We were lucky he had left through the door instead of through a window, as some bears are inclined. To gain entrance the black grizzly had pulled three-quarter-inch bolt heads through a two by four barring the door.

Once a bear finds he can get into a cabin and find good things to eat, it will continue to break into cabins. Bud and a young man, Harry Sjoberg, who, with his brother Ron and a cousin from Sweden, were helping Bud build a cabin on land we homesteaded at Cobb Lake, trailed the black grizzly to its den after a light snowfall. It emerged ready to fight. That fine trophy, made into a rug, is now on display in Harry's home in Minnesota.

It was fall, and the rat-a-tat-tat of the little chickadees picking on the frozen tallow on the window ledge as we ate breakfast started another busy day. The morning sun, brilliantly peeking over the hills by eight o'clock seemed to apologize for the nasty cold wind of the previous three days. Freeze-up was near, and it was time to change the pontoons on the airplane to wheels. The airplane would rest on the wheels for a time without going anywhere, then the skis would be mounted.

In other years Bud had flown the airplane elsewhere to changeover, but that was always a hassle: the airplane had to be left, and later retrieved, and the floats had to be left under someone else's care. This time Bud had arranged for a friend to be at Tanada to help; the friend was to bring a heavy-duty chain hoist. But neither friend nor chain hoist materialized, and we couldn't wait—there was danger of the floats freezing into the ice of the lake.

Bud anchored a winch to a stout tree and it was my job to put water-soaked boards under the pontoons as he winched the Cub out of the water an inch at a time. He had constructed a tripod to lift the airplane clear of the ground. As the plane lifted all seemed to be going well, when suddenly the pulley on the tripod broke loose, the Cub dropped to the ground, and the pulley fell on the airplane, putting a dent in the engine cowling. We both almost had heart attacks. If the pulley had hit a bit differently it could have broken the windshield. Fortunately, no real damage was done.

A wind came up and we dragged heavy driftwood logs under the airplane wings in order to tie it down. Before Bud was finished tying the plane down I put Colin on my back and started for the cabin. It was near dark and the shoreline was icy and slippery. I was watching every step when I saw

Young fisherman with Tanada trout.

a pile of steaming fresh bear dung in the trail. I did a reverse and returned to tell Bud that I thought we had had an audience while we worked. We didn't have the rifle with us because we were virtually in our front yard. Bud glanced at the bear's calling card and in the dark boldly walked the trail over the hill to the cabin with me practically clinging to his shirt tail. He was much braver than I was. The bear must have kept going, for we didn't encounter it.

Bud figured a way of repairing his chain hoist and managed to lift the airplane and remove the floats. Then he ran into another problem; the new bolts he had bought for installing the wheel struts were too long. He solved that by using many washers until he could get the proper length bolts.

We had a saying—do, make do, or do without. It's a philosophy familiar to anyone who lives in the wilderness. We usually made do, but often we did without.

A tent used by our guests needed to be taken down, and I first folded the bedding and put it away. Earlier we had left the tent standing while we were gone for a time, and red squirrels had chewed holes in a sleeping bag and scattered feathers all directions. Keno stood looking into the empty tent, probably wondering why Bud was taking away his dog house; he had taken possession, abandoning his own warm house. He moped about once the tent was knocked down, but by evening had resigned himself to his own house again. While cleaning up I had tossed a pair of Bud's heavy wool socks out the door, intending to carry them to the washroom. When I went to pick them up they were gone. I looked at Keno's nest under a tree where he lay looking innocent and saw sticking out from under a black paw the toe of a gray wool sock. He was insulted when I asked him to move, but I carried away two warm socks all covered with dog hair. He had become an important gentleman of leisure since retiring as leader of a working dog team, and he demonstrated his importance in various ways.

The sawmill blade was out of line and needed to be taken to town for repairs before Bud could saw more lumber. He didn't need the Jeep at the sawmill for power for some time, so he drove it in four-wheel-drive part way to the south end

Bud with hunter and trophies, 1961.

of the lake and walked back to the boat and crossed the lake to home. We planned one last trip to Slana before the lake froze over—I was to steer the Jeep while Bud towed it with the Weasel.

It was exciting to start out on a trip. The lake had been calm when we went to bed the previous night, but we awoke to a stiff breeze. The starting rope broke on the outboard motor with the first pull, and our trip appeared to be in jeopardy. Bud had a rope handy to hand-wind onto the flywheel, but that took time, and each time he tried he had to row out from shore. If the outboard didn't start, the waves tossed the boat back onto the beach. It started third try. But there were tiny whitecaps on the lake. "You want to wait?" he asked me.

"I'll leave it up to you," I said, knowing he would choose to go. We both knew a strong wind could blow for three to five days, and we didn't want to go through the hassle of getting ready to leave again.

It was a thrilling crossing. Bud expertly quartered into each swell, and the Aluma-Craft rode high in the water, with an occasional spray showering us. When we reached the far shore I turned to Bud and we both laughed with relief. Both of us had been thinking the same thoughts.

It took us all day to tow the Jeep to the Nabesna Road. We could have walked faster. Mr. Jones, Keno, and Colin slept most of the way. At the road we parked the Weasel and drove on to our Rufus Creek cabin. Strangely, that night both of us dreamed of once-again mushing a dog team across endless miles of rough tundra and sidehill trails. Mail at Slana, a few supplies, and we were ready to return home to start the long winter.

## XX

## BUILDING A BUSINESS

Four inches of snow fell at Tanada Lake while we were on the mail and supply run to Slana, and it changed the world to a lovely clean white, breaking the monotony of the dull brown and leafless landscape. When we arrived back at the lake in the Weasel we saw where an otter had left a wide trough as it had pushed itself through the deep snow; ptarmigan had left their distinctive three-toed prints where they had fed; and fresh caribou tracks made clear that these graceful deer were also around. The cleated tracks of the Weasel were the only visual evidence of man.

It was cozy and warm inside the weasel so babe and I waited while Bud carried the first load of stuff to the boat. He was gone so long that Colin and I had to follow to investigate, thinking he was working on the outboard motor. I hoped we wouldn't have to row home. We found him chopping ice along the shore so we could get the boat to open water.

The outboard motor started after a minor hassle. A slight breeze at our backs helped push us along, it wasn't especially cold, and our lake was beautiful in the blue semi-darkness. Then came a jarring crash that quickly brought us to reality. For a bewildering second we didn't know what had happened, then we realized that we had crashed head-on into an ice bridge. Luckily it was thin enough that the boat had forced an opening, and we didn't upset. It was close enough to dark that neither of us had seen the dark

An unhappy guide after the grizzley tore up his camp.

ice, and we hadn't expected the lake to freeze over so early. Bud managed to break the rest of the ice with the oars, and we passed again into open water. We ran slowly for the balance of the five miles, fearing another crash into ice.

Our log cabin nestled under a blanket of snow was a welcome sight. Fresh snow on the wings of the plane had to be swept off. During our slow cruise down the lake I wondered how many years my nerves would hold out; the crash into the ice gave me something to think about, and it seemed I always had plenty to worry about; Bud overdue when flying was the worst, but it became such a common occurrence that I almost got used to it.

I had a more current hassle: Keno had leaped into the boat and made a direct landing on a dozen eggs, which ran all over our mail, including the new magazines.

Within a few days the lake froze over, and, without a wind, the ice was as smooth as glass. The black and white mountains and dark spruce trees reflected so clearly in the ice that it seemed like calm open water. On our side of the lake near shore three goldeneye ducks swam around and around in a tiny patch of open water, apparently trying to keep it from freezing. I hoped they were wise enough to leave for warmer climates while they still had enough water for their long half-running half-flying takeoffs. I saw a small flock of ducks flying across the lake one morning and wondered how many had been frozen into the ice during unwary sleep.

We had a pressure cooker, and canned our moose meat in tin cans. Bud had hung meat from a late hunt that we planned to can in a shed, leaving the door open for good air circulation. There the meat aged to make it more tender. With the meat still in the shed Bud flew to Slana for the mail one day. I went to the hilltop to see if the plane was returning when I thought it was due. I carried binoculars, as was my habit, and while at the lookout point I glassed the countryside. There, half a mile away, on an open flat, was a huge grizzly bear. It appeared to be scrounging frozen blueberries.

I returned to the house and kept the rifle loaded and ready by the door, and kept a wary eye open for the bear.

Keno gave no indication he had seen the bear, and I kept him in the house. I was happy when Bud came winging home with the little Cub.

Bud was sure the bear would smell the moose meat, and that it would attempt to get a free meal during the dark of night. He closed the door of the shed to slow the bear down a bit, knowing it could easily break through anyway. If that happened, the noise would alert us. He tied Keno to a tree by our back door, expecting that he would bark if the bear came into the yard.

The bear didn't come that night. We assumed it hadn't smelled the meat, or that it happened to be a bear that went about its business without trespassing—some bears are that way. Nevertheless, in case the bear changed its mind, Bud tied Keno out the second night.

That night we heard Keno let out two loud "Woof, woofs," and then all was quiet. Bud jumped out of bed and pulled the door open just in time to see the big grizzly walk by within a few feet of the house. Keno was gone. His chain was still tied to the tree.

"Beat it!" Bud yelled to the bear, and, strangely, it disappeared into the darkness. Bud then lit the Coleman lantern and spent the rest of the night seeing the frequent reflection of the bear's eyes from the outer circle of lantern light. The big animal remained in the bushes, without attempting to get into the meat shed. Twice Bud shot a couple of rounds into the air with his rifle, aiming well above the reflection of the eyes. Each time the eyes disappeared for a time, then returned.

At daylight the bear was gone. Keno had also disappeared. Bud called and called, but Keno didn't appear. There was no evidence that the bear had anything to do with the dog's disappearance, but the circumstances were suspicious.

Late that afternoon Bud went to get something out of a storage tent and while he was there a sheepish Keno crawled out from under a cot. Malemutes aren't known for bravery around bears—they prefer that humans deal with them.

Surprisingly, that bear didn't return.

We lost Keno that winter. We went for a six week trip to the Lower 48 in January and February, leaving Keno with friends who wanted to use him as a lead dog in training two young dogs to pull a sled. Keno adjusted and seemed content, they said. But he got loose one night and disappeared. He must have been heading home, and he got hungry. About a week after he got loose he tried to get into a meat cache, and the owners, thinking it was a bear, shot and wounded him. He left, trailing blood, and died on the Nabesna Road, where a friend found and recognized him as Bud's pal. We missed him for a long time.

While living at Tanada Lake we were rarely ill. Sometimes we had colds if we were exposed to others, but that was about the extent of our illnesses. Once Bud got a toothache. He tried to ignore it, but it abscessed, and he decided he had best get himself to a dentist. The nearest was at Palmer, a 250-mile drive, one-way. The dentist pulled the tooth. He kept Bud all afternoon until finally the bleeding stopped, then he told Bud not to sneeze or blow his nose, or the bleeding might restart. He told Bud to come back in the morning.

"To hell with it," Bud said to himself, and he drove most of the night, to where the airplane was parked on the Nabesna Road. He flew home as soon as it was light. He tossed away the pain pills the dentist had sold him, and the tooth cavity healed without further problem.

Bud bought a second weasel and with much work put it in good shape. He drove it into a valley between Sheep and Grizzly Lake during sheep season. It was easy terrain for the big tracked vehicle, and it worked well. After his client killed a trophy sheep, Bud moved the Weasel to the Jacksina River where he had frequently seen a fine trophy grizzly. The same client collected that grizzly. Bud left the Weasel and camp while he flew the client out.

Later, with Husty Sanford, a local Indian assistant guide, Bud went to collect the camp and the Weasel. While crossing the Jacksina River a rock got under the track and broke something. The two men built a tripod and winched the Weasel out of the river, leaving it parked on the bank. The Jacksina overflowed its banks, washing the valuable Weasel

Bud with Fred Packer and Trophies, 1964.

downstream, and turning it upside down. There it remained until winter, and daily for some time Bud flew to it, landed, and chipped frozen sand and ice away from the wrecked vehicle until he managed to remove the engine piecemeal. He flew the parts back to Tanada Lake and rebuilt the engine. Later he bought a new Weasel hull and rebuilt it, using the rebuilt engine in it.

Bud continued to build up the lodge. He completed a 14 × 18-foot living room, which we thoroughly enjoyed. He added a 10 × 10-foot log trophy room-office, which we used for a time as a bedroom until we completed a third cabin. He built a guest cabin out of plywood that he hauled in with the Weasel towing a sled in winter. He varnished it on the inside, and painted the plywood floor. Insulated, it was warm and cozy with an airtight wood burning stove. We set up five cots in it for our guests.

We called the third cabin The Honeymoon Cabin, because the first guests to use it were newly married, and came to Tanada Lake to hide away from work associates who had planned an old fashioned shivaree. We eventually moved our bed and belongings to this neat little cabin. It sat on the hillside with a big picture window overlooking the lake, and I was happy to make the move. I had become irritated at bumping my head on the huge trophy caribou that hung on the wall at the foot of our bed, and Bud was irritated with me every time he returned home from a trip and found clothing hung to dry on his record-book caribou trophy!

Finally we were ready for business, and we started to advertise in the leading sporting magazines. Our adds read something like this:

**TANADA LAKE LODGE—Big game hunting and fishing, specializing in Dall sheep hunts of 10, 15, and 20 days. Moose, caribou, grizzly, and black bear. Bud Conkle, registered guide, Slana, Alaska.**

With recommendations from our many satisfied clients, by the mid-1950's we were fully booked for two and three years in advance.

The great Wrangell Mountains produced trophy Dall rams for our hunters. All guides and assistant guides who worked for Bud were instructed to not allow their hunters to shoot any Dall ram with a horn curl that measured less than 38 inches. There were plenty to choose from of that size and larger. The largest number of rams killed by our hunters in one season was 12, and all were fine old trophies—rams that had little time left of their lives. Bud set out hunters and guides in spike camps in many areas. Bud did all the flying, and he guided on some of the hunts. I did the cooking and made up the grocery boxes for the spike camps.

Our fall hunting seasons lasted but about two months, but they seemed longer. We worked from five a.m. until late night nearly every day. During evenings hunting stories unfolded around campfires in spike camps, or at the dinner table in our main camp, making it an interesting time with interesting people.

There was a constant need for supplies. It was my job to drive to Anchorage or Valdez in our new Ford station wagon to do the shopping. Sometimes I drove to Anchorage and met incoming clients at the airport, or sometimes they flew to much closer Gulkana where I would meet them. Then I often drove them back to Gulkana or Anchorage when their hunts ended. Frequently Bud flew the airplane with a load while I drove the Nabesna Road. In the spring or after heavy rains the creeks often ran over their banks, and there were planks on hand, and it was up to whoever drove the road to put the planks in place and carefully drive across. I was pleased that I could do this. Most of the creeks had gravel bottom, and if the water wasn't too deep I could ford them without the planks.

If I didn't arrive on time, Bud flew over, he would see that I was stuck, and he would land on the nearest lake and walk to help me. At the time no one lived on the Nabesna Road, and often days went by without a single vehicle driving it. When I had a flat tire I had to jack up the wheel and change it.

Bud bought his aviation fuel at Valdez. He would buy three 55-barrels at a time and haul them in the Jeep trailer to Jack Lake, then he would pack five gallon cans a half

246

Hide of Grizzley that mauled gold miner, Knut Peterson, in 1949.

mile to the airplane and gas it up, and with the airplane haul gasoline in five gallon cans to Tanada Lake.

We had some nightmarish trips on icy roads over the years. Once the Jeep spun out on Thompson Pass, the high pass that the highway crosses in the coastal mountains on the route to Valdez. We were pulling the trailer with three full barrels of gasoline. The Jeep was in four-wheel-drive, with chains on both rear wheels. Bud used the little hatchet he always carried and chopped ice down to bare gravel, making a trail for the left wheels. He put an emergency chain on the front wheel, and darned if he didn't drive on over the summit. I couldn't believe it. It took the better part of that day.

A couple of times I was with Bud when he had to drive with the Jeep door open and one foot along the edge of the road to feel the edge: it was that or risk driving into a snow bank because blowing snow had reduced visibility. Other times I remember being in blowing snow on Thompson Pass, following the tanker truck of old-timer Jack Wallace. Jack would follow snow plows, and we followed him. All we could see was the occasional flash of his tail lights when he hit his brakes.

Looking back, I think perhaps the years of struggle were the best. We had little but hope and ambition, and every little accomplishment loomed large. We did enjoy the successful years, but by then we were somehow under obligation—we had to continue what we had started. We had to produce for our clients. We weren't quite so relaxed, nor were we quite so young.

## XXI

## AIRPLANE ADVENTURES

We couldn't have built our guiding and lodge business to the extent we did without an airplane. Wings proved to be the key to our success.

Colin was not yet two years old when he climbed into the baggage compartment of the J-3 Cub when Bud was getting ready to fly a fisherman out to Jack Lake. He curled up as low as he could get and hung onto the crossbar and coaxed his dad to allow him to go. Daddy said ok. Mama wrung her hands and paced the beach when they were ten minutes overdue on the return flight. The 40 minutes they were gone had seemed like hours. And then when Bud finally arrived and gently eased the Cub down onto the lake and I rushed to open the door Colin seemed so tiny sitting in the rear seat with the seat belt fastened across his lap. That was the first time he had flown without being on my lap, but, of course, it was only a start. He flew many an hour with his father over the years, and he could handle the airplane and beach it like an expert by the time he was twelve years old. He could even taxi it on the water at that age. Colin had a private pilot's license when he was eighteen years old, and a commercial license a few years later.

In 1958 Bud flew the J-3 Cub to Fairbanks for an engine overhaul. He was offered a fair deal on a trade-in for a new airplane, so after a visit to our now-friendly-banker, we became the proud owners of a brand new Piper Super Cub. Our growing business warranted the investment.

Wolf hides taken for bounty.

Our lovely little J-3 Cub N42126 came to a sad end. It was purchased by Paul Tovey, a fine young Fairbanksan. Not long after he bought it, Tovey and his passenger were lost while aerial hunting wolves. The crashed plane wasn't found until the following spring when the snow melted away from it. Tovey and his gunner probably died on impact.

Years later Colin, flying as a commercial pilot, flew over the wreckage of that airplane and wondered about it. He didn't realize it was the little J-3 his father had owned when he was a boy until sometime in the late 1970's, when he read an account of the long cold-weather search for Tovey and his airplane, describing the site of the crash.

The better performance of the new Super Cub, its greater speed, and ability to haul heavier loads were good reasons for us to trade up. N84464D proved to be a good investment over the years, and with it Bud was able to go places and do things that would have been impossible with the little J-3 Cub.

For example, in the summer of 1960 Bud used the Super Cub on floats to spot salmon for the *Valiant Maid*, a commercial seine boat fished by Ed Bilderbeck in Prince William Sound. The income from that one summer gave us enough to pay off the bank loan for the new airplane.

That summer wasn't without its excitement. One night while the crew slept a sudden wind tore the airplane loose from the *Valiant Maid*. When Bud awoke and dashed up on deck the airplane was gone and out of sight. It was dark, and the spotlight on the boat didn't pick it up on the shore where everyone expected to see it being pounded to junk. The airplane had drifted around a rocky point and when found next morning at daylight it was undamaged and serenely floating on quiet water in a sheltered cover.

Near the end of Bud's season of spotting fish in Prince William Sound and when we had no more fishing clients at Tanada Lake, Colin and I flew to Cordova to spend a few days and fly home with him. Cordova was clear when we took off headed for home, with lifting fog reported at Valdez. Prince William Sound was calm and we enjoyed the beautiful scenery until a blanket of fog forced Bud to land and taxi into what he thought was Jack Bay. It wasn't. The rocky shores of the bay we were in would have wrecked the Super Cub if a wind had come up while we were there.

Bud taxied back out of the bay and found that the fog had lifted enough for him to take off and fly close to the water. We spotted Shoup Glacier, 12 miles west of Valdez, and then the fog forced us to land again. Bud taxied toward Valdez Harbor, and was surprised when we crossed waves created by an airplane—our own. We had taxied in a circle. He shut off the engine and got a heading from harbor sounds at Valdez. Again he taxied slowly through the milky fog, and was startled when the spent wake of a passing ship rocked the airplane. Again Bud shut off the engine, and we listened to the sounds of the departing ship. How close? Too close, whatever the distance. We later learned that it had been a large ship. If we had been in front of it instead of behind, we would have been run down.

When we finally arrived at a dock in Valdez we tied the airplane and walked to Max Well's store in town.

"Where did you come from?" Max asked. He was astounded to learn we had just flown from Cordova. Valdez had been fogged in for three days, with no one flying.

Bud also hunted wolves with the Super Cub. During those Territorial years many pilots made good money at this business, and it lasted until after statehood, when aerial hunting of wolves in Alaska was halted. The $50 bounty paid for each wolf, plus the fine pelt, which could bring $100 or more in those years, was a welcome supplement to our meager income. This practice helped to keep wolves under control, and benefitted moose, sheep, and caribou numbers. No one wanted to see the wolves exterminated, and they weren't. Wolves reproduce rapidly, and they are wily adversaries. When a pilot flew over a lone wolf or a pack he could instantly tell if they had been shot at by another aerial hunter; a pack would scatter, or a lone wolf would dodge when a plane came near. Once they reached cover there was little chance of flushing them again.

One of Bud's exciting aerial wolf hunting adventures occurred with Walter Sinn, a Sergeant with the Territorial Police who flew as his gunner. Using Bud's notes and my diary I wrote that story under Bud's name and it appeared in the November 1985 issue of *ALASKA MAGAZINE*. Outdoors Editor Jim Rearden wrote an editor's note, providing perspective. Here is that story as it appeared in print, including the editor's note:

1958
GHOST WOLF OF THE COLEEN
By Bud Conkle

*This is an adventure story from Alaska's colorful past. The author, Clement M. "Bud" Conkle, a 38-year resident of Alaska, died February 26, 1985, at the age of 73. He was a well-known guide and bush pilot, who, with his wife LeNora, built Tanada Lake Lodge in the early 1950's. Bud was still active as a pilot and a guide at the time of his death.*

*Aerial hunting of coyotes and other predators is still a common sport in some western states, but aerial hunting of Alaska's wolves for sport (or profit) ended in 1971. The only aerial hunting allowed for Alaska's wolves today is for predator control, and it is done mostly by state employees in specific areas under tightly controlled authorizations issued by the Alaska Board of Game.*

*When Bud Conkle made his Coleen River wolf hunt in 1958, Alaska was still a Territory, and the U.S. Fish and Wildlife Service managed Alaska's wildlife. Wolves were regarded as undesirable—a menace to moose, caribou and sheep. The USFWS waged a continual war against them using poison, aerial shooting and trapping. The Territory paid a $50 bounty for each wolf killed by a resident, there was no closed season on wolves, and every effort was made to reduce numbers of the big predator. Permits were issued by the USFWS for aerial wolf hunting, and almost any responsible resident pilot could get one simply by applying for it.—Ed.*

The turbulence was growing more severe as I throttled back the Super Cub and started to descend, hoping to find more stable air at a lower altitude on February 26, 1958. At about 1,500 feet the going wasn't quite so rough, although we still had strong headwinds.

Walter Sinn and I had left Fairbanks 30 minutes earlier in almost perfect weather—about 10 degrees above zero with bright sunlight and no wind. We planned to fly 140 miles north to Fort Yukon, just inside the Arctic Circle, where we were to headquarter for an Arctic wolf hunt.

Happy hunters with moose.

Walt, a sergeant with the Alaska Territorial Police, had considerable experience in hunting wolves from the air. He is a fine shot with either a shotgun or rifle. I'm a professional big game guide and bush pilot, and I have done a lot of aerial wolf hunting in the years I've been guiding and flying in Alaska. During the previous spring I had done considerable wolf hunting in the area we were bound for, and I knew the country quite well.

We both had sleeping bags—Walt sat on his like a fox on a beaver house. Also aboard were 15 gallons of extra gasoline in cans, a rifle, Walt's Browning automatic shotgun, five boxes of No. 4 buckshot, emergency rations and a plumber's firepot and warm-up cover for the plane. The firepot and warm-up cover are standard for winter bush flying in the North, as aircraft engines have to be preheated before starting in the normal winter temperatures ranging from 10 above to sometimes 35 or 40 degrees below zero. Any colder than that and most of us prefer to wait until another day.

When we left the mountains and arrived over the Yukon River flats, we were out of most of the wind. The high peaks of the Brooks Range began to take shape through the haze to the north. We would be over those peaks tomorrow if the weather allowed. We landed at Fort Yukon for gas and to arrange for lodging at the local roadhouse before continuing north to look for wolves.

At Fort Yukon I picked up three months' back mail for an old trapper. I had met the man the previous year at his cabin on the Coleen River, 140 air miles from Fort Yukon. He told me that he had spent 40 years in the area trapping and prospecting, coming out about once a year, usually in the spring, for supplies. He used to make the 200-mile trip by riverboat, but in later years the local bush pilot flew him in and out.

Leaving Fort Yukon, we flew up the Porcupine River to its confluence with the Coleen. We flew over several large herds of caribou and a good many moose. We saw old wolf sign, but much of it was so mixed with the caribou trails as to make trailing from the air almost impossible. We had long since left the Fairbanks banana belt and noticed that

255

the wing thermometer held steady at 15 degrees below zero, which meant it was probably 25 below on the ground.

The previous year, while wolf hunting near the headwaters of the Coleen, we got into a pack of 11 wolves, managing to make one pass on a black one, which we collected, before the rest of them left the river and ran into the timber. I had glimpsed a light-colored wolf as we made the pass on the black—it was among the first to get into the timber. We weren't able to run any of them back out on the open river, which can sometimes be accomplished by circling a quarter of a mile away or so. Occasionally the drone of the engine will drive them back into the open, but it doesn't always work, and it didn't this time. We concluded that these wolves were educated. But I couldn't forget the white one—I called it the Ghost Wolf of the Coleen. I sure would have liked to have had his skin.

It was late by the time we circled the trapper's cabin. There was no smoke, and we began to wonder if the old fellow had set his last trap. We landed and snowshoed to the cabin and found the door chained from the outside, with a note saying he'd gone upriver to another cabin and that he expected to be back around the first of March. The note was dated the previous month. We left his mail and flew back to Fort Yukon.

February 27 produced 20-below zero and a 20-mph wind from the northeast. Flying in that kind of wind is tough at best; making low passes on wolves in brush country is just not a good idea. We decided to fly up the Yukon River, which flows just about east to west at this point, and perhaps get out of some of the wind.

Several hundred miles and six hours later we returned to Fort Yukon, wolfless and beat.

February 28 dawned with little wind and a nice even 20-below-zero on the ground and 10 below in the air. We got an early start and made a long sweep across the east fork of the Chandalar River, then flew back to the headwaters of the Sheenjek River, which lies between the Chandalar and the Coleen. We had been in the air about three hours when we were flying down the Sheenjek.

"There goes a wolf on the river," Walt yelled.

I throttled back and circled the timber in order to try to haze the wolf toward the opening in the center of the river. on the second pass we saw another gray wolf. Both wolves had jumped up on the bank and were standing on the edge of the timber on a bend in the river—hardly the place for a pass.

I continued circling over the timbered side, and as I came around the turn on the near side to the wolves I noticed that they didn't seem to be worried about us. In fact, one wolf appeared to be playing with something, tossing it into the air and catching it. Finally, after we had made the fourth turn, the playboy trotted out to the middle of the river.

I throttled back and made an upwind pass on him, dropping quarter flaps and slowing to about 50 mph. Walt got off two shots with his shotgun as we approached to within 15 yards of the wolf. The wolf had just started to get under way and was running at a pretty good clip when Walt nailed him. He fell and didn't move.

We landed nearby on the frozen river. The object the wolf had been playing with was the jawbone of a caribou; it was lying beside the wolf. We got the wolf skin peeled off quickly and were soon back in the air. We couldn't locate the other wolf. It was late, so we called it a day and headed for Fort Yukon.

March 1 was clear and windy, 15 degrees below zero. We decided to fly up the Big Black River which runs into the Porcupine River northeast of Fort Yukon. We saw considerable wolf sign near the Alaska-Yukon border. We flew over an estimated 5,000 caribou, but after five hours of wolfless flying, we turned back to Fort Yukon.

March 2 had bright sun, calm winds and 20-below-zero temperature—ideal. We flew up the Porcupine River to the Sheenjek, then up the Sheenjek to the mouth of the Koness River, and over the ridge to the Coleen, then down the Colen to its confluence with the Porcupine, and then followed the Porcupine back to Fort Yukon.

We were 10 miles from the mouth of the Koness when I spotted a gray wolf ahead on the river. I was able to throttle back, lose altitude, and close in behind the wolf just off the river. Just as we were closing to shooting range, the running

Bud, center, with two satisfied clients.

Hunters with trophies.

wolf neared a bend in the river and ran in close to shore. I was forced to pull up to clear a patch of high willows, making the shot for Walt a little farther than he liked. It was a clean miss, and before we could make a second pass the wolf had left the river as if someone had spilled turpentine on his rear. We flew around for 20 minutes, but were unable to locate it. We landed to look for a sign that we might have hit it, but found nothing.

We took to the air again and, half a mile from where we had jumped the gray wolf, spotted a caribou on the riverbank that had apparently been killed by wolves. Only parts of the hindquarters had been eaten.

We were upriver a couple of miles, looking for the wolves that had killed the caribou, when Walt called, "There goes a black wolf."

I slowed the plane and turned to lose altitude to come up behind it. As I turned I saw a second black wolf about 100 yards ahead of the first. Both wolves stayed on the river, which was wide at this point. I came upriver low and slow for the pass on the first wolf. He was scratching and running for all he was worth, and we could see the muscles working in his legs and back. As Walt shot, the wolf stumbled, caught himself and veered to the side. I continued flying up the river, just off the ice, at about 50 mph. We closed on the second wolf and at the shot it went down to stay.

We returned to where we had shot the first wolf, landed, and found blood in the tracks. After following the tracks for more than a mile, the blood spots stopped and the wolf hadn't slowed a bit. We concluded that he was only slightly wounded, returned and skinned the other wolf, and then took off for the Coleen.

We saw some wolf sign after we reached the Coleen, but no wolves. There were a good many caribou near the mouth of the Coleen where it flows into the Porcupine River. We flew upstream and found a fresh wolf track going upstream. We followed the track for about five miles and then spotted a wolf on the river far ahead. The river was wide and straight. We dropped to within 15 feet of the ice and closed from behind. Until we were within 50 yards the wolf displayed no alarm. When he realized we were after him, it was too late; Walt nailed him with one shot. We landed close by and skinned the animal on the spot. The pelt was dark and exceptionally well furred.

The day was about gone, so we took off and headed toward Fort Yukon. It was getting quite cloudy, but the ceiling remained fairly high. As it turned dark I switched on the running lights and climbed to 2,000 feet. We could see the beacon light at Fort Yukon 75 miles away. I set a straight course, and we landed less than an hour later.

March 3 brought light snow. We fire-potted the engine and waited an hour. The weather started to lift, so we took off and headed for the Coleen. We searched carefully, but though we knew there were wolves about, we saw none. By the time we neared the headwaters of the Coleen at the 5,000-foot level in the foothills of the Brooks Range, most all game had disappeared except for tracks left by a lone wolverine.

It was late afternoon, the weather was blustery, our gas was getting low, we had seen no wolves to shoot at, and it was the last day of our hunt. We felt pretty low as we headed back down river toward Fort Yukon.

Twenty minutes later Walt yelled, "There goes a wolf way up ahead on the river."

I was too high and had to turn back and lose altitude. As we came back down river, low, I saw the wolf, far ahead. It was really making tracks. There was a clump of willows on a sand bar in the middle of the river, and as we approached to within about 40 yards of this clump, a big, almost pure white wolf streaked ahead of our low-flying plane. I kicked the rudder left in order to put the wolf on our right, at the same time yelling to Walt, "Get the white one."

He couldn't hear me with the wind howling in the open door at 60 mph, but he saw the white wolf and fired at it as we went past. The wolf leaped to the side, and it appeared the shot was a clean miss. But at that speed and 15 feet off the deck with a river bend coming up fast and tall spruces lining the banks, you don't have time to stare at an object very long and stay alive.

We figured we had missed that one. Then, just as we were closing in on the gray wolf that we had first spotted, it made a break for the timber. I couldn't make a pass on it without flying into the trees and I had to pull up. The timber was sparse here away from the river, and we located the wolf again, but couldn't get in low enough for a decent shot. At one point in this exciting chase, the wolf ran through a bunch of about 50 caribou, and for a time it was a case of airplane chasing wolf and wolf chasing caribou. Caribou and wolf dashed into the timber so thick that upon completing a turn we had lost track of the wolf. After 20 minutes of searching and circling, we gave up.

It was now late and a few snow showers started. The low light level and snow created white-out conditions. If it hadn't been for the trees along the river we couldn't have known where the river ice was.

I couldn't leave without landing and at least having a close look at where we had shot at the white wolf. I made three turns over the river near where the animal had been, finally settled for a place on the river that looked well protected from the wind, and set her down.

We got out and started looking around. "There it is, over there!" Walt shouted.

The white wolf was stretched out on the ice, stone dead. We had flown over it several times without either of us seeing it. It was so white against the white background that we could scarcely see it at 30 yards.

The wolf was a large male, about 130 pounds, and the pelt was in fine condition. He appeared to be very old and almost all of his teeth were worn to the gums. The upper fangs on the right side of the jaw were broken clear off. We surmised that the other wolf was the white one's mate, with the female doing all of the killing, because this old, nearly toothless wolf probably couldn't kill big game. He may have been in his last year, for a toothless wolf would have a lot of trouble eating raw meat.

We weren't going to flood the market with our collection of wolf pelts from this hunt, but Walt and I congratulated each other. We felt the white wolf was a fitting climax to a fine wolf hunt. He had flown five days and a total of 30 hours. We had seen a number of wolves and collected a few. We had flown over many thousands of caribou and a good

Bud Conkle with sheep, moose, caribou and goat trophies taken in 1963

John Kreps with nice grizzley.

many moose. We had flown over and come to know some of the wildest country under the American flag.

We felt good as we flew down the Coleen River in the stormy darkness with the welcoming beacon light at Fort Yukon guiding us in for a safe landing. We had as a trophy the Ghost Wolf of the Coleen River.

Bud had the lovely white skin of that big male wolf made into a rug, and he hung it on display in our trophy room at Tanada Lake Lodge.

# XXII

## AIRPLANE THROUGH THE ICE

Bud's pride and joy was his new Piper Supercub. He babied it so much that there were times I was almost jealous. If only he thought as much of me. . . .

To say he was chagrined when that lovely almost-new airplane broke through the ice at Tanada Lake is putting it mildly. From Bud's notes and my diary I wrote an article in Bud's name on this to us momentous and sad event, and it was published in the December 1985 issue of *ALASKA FLYING*. This is the way it appeared in print:

HINDSIGHT
Super Cub Through the Ice
By Bud Conkle

Crunch! Whoosh! With the sickening sound of breaking ice, my new Super Cub dropped through the ice on Tanada Lake in the Wrangell Mountains.

It was early December 1959 and the ice had been four inches thick when my wife LeNora, son Colin, and I had left for a two-week stay in Anchorage. It was so cold when we left I was sure the ice would grow thicker every day. I didn't know that a warm spell would come in our absence, and balmy winds helped melt the lake ice. Subsequent frigid temperatures re-froze the surface.

If I had any doubts about the ice giving way under my plane I would have taken the precaution of bouncing the

265

Outdoor transportation, the old and new at Tanada Lake.

wheels on the ice, then flying back to see if there was any water in my tracks. Any experienced bush pilot knows enough to test the ice before landing. I could also, of course, put skis on my plane. Most likely skis would have supported it.

It was a sunny day without wind and I had plenty of things I should have been doing besides flying. I should have utilized the calm day to change from wheels to skis, for instance. But...

I asked Junior Duffy from Duffy's Roadhouse at Slana if he would like to accompany me to Tanada lake where I was going to check on our hunting and fishing lodge. The bears should have been in hibernation, but a cabin-wrecking grizzly had been around all summer, so we were closely watching our buildings.

Duffy was pleased to go and rushed to get ready. I saw no reason to fly there with an empty airplane, so I loaded a few cans and bags of groceries that freezing wouldn't hurt. After Duffy was settled in the back seat with his seat belt fastened, I put a 60-pound bag of sugar on his lap.

I landed farther out from my normal ski pattern because I knew my brakes would be ineffective on the smooth ice. I figured I had ample room to roll to the shoreline and my tie-down spot. I knew I had figured wrong when I heard the totally unexpected sound of breaking ice!

Down went the Super Cub. I yelled to Duffy, "We've gotta get out of here!"

Luckily the wings spread the weight of the plane across the ice and kept it from sinking. In no time at all I unfastened my seat belt, climbed out the side door and onto the wing. I scooted across the ice to shore. When I got there I looked back and saw no sign of Duffy. All I saw was the awful sight of airplane wings and broken ice. I ran back across the ice, fervently hoping it would hold my running weight, and onto the wing.

A wet head emerged from the plane, with a hand groping for a hold. Duffy was disoriented. I grabbed the outstretched hand, pulled him onto the wing and almost dragged him across the ice to shore. He was soaked and shivering, with teeth chattering, from the icy dunking. I had bailed out so fast I hadn't gotten wet.

Duffy wasn't very familiar with flying, and it had happened so suddenly. Too, he trusted me as a competent pilot. As a result he hadn't gotten his seat belt unfastened right away. He fought to get rid of the sack of sugar on his lap, and the water poured in FAST. I was thankful that my passenger didn't drown.

Soon we had a fire going in the lodge, with Duffy wrapped in blankets. A log cabin holds the heat well once the logs and contents are warm, but it takes ages to get warm when it has been below zero for days. We stayed at the lodge only long enough to eat, get Duffy into dry clothes and warmed up.

We started walking. I didn't want to be rescued and had always told LeNora to give me enough time to walk out if I was ever overdue.

Duffy didn't want to stay at the lodge alone, which would have been more practical. It didn't take long to realize I had made a poor decision by letting him walk the 12 miles to Nabesna Road. I was in good physical condition; he was not. I had to stop every few miles to build a fire so he could rest.

The temperature was around zero, so it wasn't uncomfortably cold. We made it to a log cabin around midnight. We had no sleeping bags, but managed to drowse close to the stove. I stayed warm getting wood all night.

Next morning, when we still hadn't returned from our "two hour" flight, LeNora phoned to alert Cleo McMahan that I was overdue. He started a search.

Meanwhile, I had left Duffy at the cabin with plenty of firewood and started walking to Slana, a distance of 26 miles. I had gone only a few miles when McMahan flew over low. There was nowhere to land his Cub, so he throttled back and hollered that he'd send a car for us.

He then flew over our cabin at Slana and yelled to LeNora and Colin, "They're walking out." He went to land on the Tok Highway at Duffy's Tavern to let them know we were safe. They sent a car for us.

Cleo told us later that on arrival at Tanada Lake he had

spotted the wings of my airplane level with the ice. He wasn't sure if we had gotten out, as he saw no smoke from the lodge chimney. Seeing the tracks leading around the lake, he followed them to the road. The snow was crusted and he couldn't tell if two people had walked away from the submerged plane or just one. He was certainly relieved when he learned we were both safe.

We may have been able to salvage the Cub ourselves with the help of our many friends had we done so immediately. But the insurance company told us to leave it as it was for evaluation. After a few days, they sent out Art Smith, a salvage expert. By then the plane was well frozen in.

Glen Gregory also came to help with the salvage and Cleo McMahan flew in whenever he could to help. We put them all up at the lodge and LeNora stayed busy cooking for us and heating water to thaw the ice.

With my chain saw I cut through the ice in a complete circle around the frozen-in plane. We then turned the whole chunk, plane and ice, so the tail faced the bank with the nose into the prevailing wind. Everyone made many tiring trips carrying buckets of hot water from the lodge. We poured hot water over all portions of the plane connected to the ice, and with ice chisels chipped as close as we dared without damaging the fabric.

Three days of steady work freed the aircraft from the ice. I got up several times every night to haul hot water to keep it from re-freezing. We set a tripod up over the plane when it was free from the exterior ice, raised it out of the eight inches of ice and six feet of water, and pulled it to shore.

The interior and wings were full of ice and water, so the chore wasn't over. We wrapped the airplane in all the blankets and sleeping bags we could find, then built a fire on both sides. We piped heat from the fires into the cocooned Cub with lengths of stove pipe. We kept the fires burning continuously for two days and nights. Art drilled holes in all the right places to drain the water. Luckily, the engine and propeller were not damaged.

The airplane was still somewhat wing heavy when Art decided it was ready for him to fly it to Fairbanks. Once there, Bachner went clear through it, draining water and

Bud Conkle with his Super Cub.

drying and refinishing as needed, and it was flying again in a couple of weeks.

That old Super Cub N8464D has flown a lot of hours, and it has been rebuilt twice since then. An old bush plane becomes a family treasure, and Colin still flies this family treasure from his home at North Pole, near Fairbanks.

# XXIII

## EPILOGUE

Our dream of building a wilderness lodge at Tanada Lake became a reality. When we started, Tanada Lake was considered to be wilderness, and bankers we asked for financial help thought we were too far away from the mainstream to attract clients.

They were wrong, of course, and we were right. Tanada Lake became a financial success. However, there is a time for everything. In the 1950's and 1960's sportsmen came from far and wide to enjoy the lodge, the hunting, and the magnificent surrounding wilderness.

The areas where Bud first conducted his guided hunts were relatively unhunted, but within a few years increasing numbers of other guides appeared in these areas, also conducting hunts. Soon Alaska's infamous "aerial hunting period" arrived, when guides with Super Cubs literally combed the finest hunting areas in Alaska from the air, landing their clients near trophy animals. This wasn't ethical hunting, and it disgusted Bud. During the same period many American businessmen got record book fever; many had never hunted and were not sportsmen. The "in" thing was to hunt in Alaska and bag a trophy that was large enough to be recorded in the Boone and Crockett *Records of North American Big Game*. These businessmen-hunters (they weren't sportsmen) wanted a fast hunt—a quick flight into the wilderness, a quick shot or two, and then they wanted to leave. The ethical and leisurely foot hunts that

Bud conducted in which enjoyment of the wilderness, pleasure at seeing game and carefully selecting a suitable trophy, with a lot of yarning around the campfire, was foreign to these hunters.

Trails that Bud blazed high in the Wrangell Mountains suddenly became well-used byways with a new type of machine—all terrain vehicles (ATV's). These inexpensive, noisy little things could go almost anywhere, and they did.

As result, Bud found it difficult to guide his clients in his old areas—the hit-and-run guides and roaring ATV's gave the hunts a feel of down-town Fairbanks. The kind of hunters Bud guided wanted a wilderness experience, and Tanada Lake and environs began to be less and less a wilderness with all such "progress."

The 1960's was a turbulent time for Alaska's guiding industry. Alaskans didn't like the new type of guide, and the legislature responded by creating a guide board that soon made major changes in the profession of guiding. Each guide was assigned one or more exclusive guiding areas, and unethical hit-and-run guides were no longer free to roam the entire state in search of easy pickings. A regulation that prohibited hunting on the same day that a hunter was airborne was enacted by the board of game, controlling the misuse of airplanes in hunting.

While all of this was going on, to escape the "quickie" hunts and to get beyond reach of the ubiquitous ATV's, Bud started flying clients into lakes far back in the Nutzotin Range—a branch of the Wrangell Mountains. One, Wolf Lake, was quite small; it took confidence and experience to land and take off from it, especially with a crosswind, or with no wind and a heavy load. Yet Bud and Colin made hundreds of landings and take-offs from it without an accident. Colin was now doing much of the flying for us at Wolf Lake, and he was every bit as capable a pilot as his father. He held a ClassA guide license and helped with the guiding.

Bud once described flying from Wolf Lake: "Pull the heel of the floats onto the sandy shore, firewall the throttle, coax the plane to its limit, pop the flaps to exchange airspeed for altitude, jump over the low trees, and pray you wouldn't hear the branches spank the underside of the floats as you head out for another load."

This tiny lake is at the foot of towering peaks where white Dall sheep live in the high mountain meadows. A pack of wolves lived near, and we named the lake for them, grateful for the many September nights on which they serenaded us and and our clients with their musical wild howls.

Bud built a sturdy log cabin and high cache at Wolf Lake. An even further change came when we bought saddle and packhorses and started using them to guide hunters into the nearby mountains. The grass grew lush around Wolf Lake, and during the hunting season the horses were content here, staked out at intervals along the shore. Tents were pitched to house our clients, guides, and horse wranglers.

Our peak years for Tanada Lake lodge were past, and we sold it. The five acres of patented land at Tanada Lake that we owned is now an inholding in the vast Wrangell-St. Elias National Park and Preserve, established in 1980. That five acres, which we had patent for as a business site on Tanada Lake, is the only land on the lake that will ever be in private hands. We sold the land and lodge to Thomas Dean, of Fairbanks, who later sold it to five professional men of Fairbanks. These men have invested much time and money in making improvements, until today Tanada Lake Lodge is a fine modern lodge. Reportedly the fishing is still fabulous.

Before we sold Tanada Lake Lodge, however, we homesteaded 160 acres on the north shore of Cobb Lake at 58-Mile on the Tok Highway. This became Eagle Trail Ranch, our base of operations for big game hunting, and where we wintered our horses. A few acres of the ranch encompass a part of the old Eagle Trail that in the early 1900's ran from Valdez to Eagle on the Yukon River. We still occasionally find artifacts of the era along this old trail. Through the 1960's during the months of March and April Bud guided hunters for polar bears in Alaska's Arctic, and took hunters to the Alaska Peninsula for Alaska's giant brown bears.

With money from the sale of Tanada Lake Lodge we built a modern two-story log home on Eagle Trail Ranch. It has all the comforts too—as long as the Witte generator operates. Running water was a real luxury after 30 years of packing water, taking a bath in a tin tub, and using an outhouse. Framed in the large windows is beautiful eternally-snow-capped Mount Sanford. From the trees that grew upon the land Bud soon built a garage, and we had an ample supply of wood for fireplace and stoves. He built two miles of road over muskeg and clay hills, and put in a bush plane landing field and a float plane base.

Bud is gone now. He died suddenly of a heart attack on February 26, 1985, at the age of 73, while cranking the starting motor of a D-4 Caterpillar. He was preparing to blade the snow off of our two miles of road. Two days previously we had returned from a three-month trip to the South 48 with our new 5th wheel trailer. At the time of his death Bud held Master Guide License No. 19, and three exclusive guiding areas were assigned to him by the Guide Licensing and Control Board.

Colin and I scattered his ashes over the land he loved and had worked so hard on for 40 years. He is now forever a part of wilderness Alaska.

With light only from flickering flames of burning logs I often sit in front of the great rock fireplace that Bud built in the trophy room at Eagle Trail Ranch. At such times, surrounded by treasured trophies and mementos, my mind often travels back to Tanada Lake—Wind on the Water—and our years there.

The memories are good.